LEADER'S M

JOHN FINNEY & FEL

SAINTS ALIVE!

LIVING LIFE IN THE SPIRIT TODAY

A NINE-WEEK COURSE FOR CHURCHES AND SMALL GROUPS

DAVID C COOK

transforming lives together

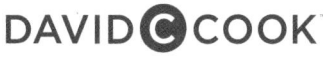

SAINTS ALIVE! LEADER'S MANUAL
Published by David C Cook
4050 Lee Vance Drive
Colorado Springs, CO 80918 U.S.A.

Integrity Music Limited, a Division of David C Cook
Brighton, East Sussex BN1 2RE, England

The graphic circle C logo is a registered trademark of David C Cook.

All rights reserved. Except for brief excerpts for review purposes,
no part of this book may be reproduced or used in any form
without written permission from the publisher.

The website addresses recommended throughout this book are offered as a resource to you. These websites are not intended in any way to be or imply an endorsement on the part of David C Cook, nor do we vouch for their content.

Unless otherwise noted, all Scripture quotations are taken from the *Holy Bible*, New Living Translation, copyright © 1996, 2007, 2015 by Tyndale House Foundation. Used by permission of Tyndale House Publishers, Inc., Carol Stream, Illinois 60188. All rights reserved. Scripture quotations marked PHILLIPS are taken from The New Testament in Modern English, Revised Edition © 1972 by J. B. Phillips. Copyright renewed © 1986, 1988 by Vera M. Phillips.

ISBN 978-0-8307-8148-5
eISBN 978-0-8307-8213-0

© 2020 John Finney and Felicity Lawson
First edition published by Moorley's Print and Publishing in 1982 ©
John Finney and Felicity Lawson, ISBN 978-0-8607-1136-0

The Team: Ian Matthews, Jennie Pollock, Jack Campbell, Susan Murdock
Cover Design: Mark Prentice at beatroot.media

Printed in the United Kingdom
Third Edition 2020

1 2 3 4 5 6 7 8 9 10

100220

CONTENTS

INTRODUCTION — **6**

SECTION 1—WHAT IS THE COURSE? — **10**
The Aims of the Course
The Structure of the Course
The Video

SECTION 2—HOW TO RUN THE COURSE — **16**
How Can the Course Be Used?
Where Do the People Come From?
Where Should It Be Held?
Who Are These People?
Approach and Atmosphere
Flexibility
Where to Meet
Food
Visual Aids
Worship
After the Course

SECTION 3—THE LEADERS — **31**
Training and Supporting Leaders
Number of Leaders

SECTION 4—BEFORE YOU START ... — **36**

INTRODUCTORY MEETING OR PARTY   39

Session 1—**RELATIONSHIPS MATTER!**   45
Human Relationships
Relationship with God
Loving and Being Loved

Session 2—**WHO IS JESUS?**   59
The Person of Jesus
The Passion
The Importance of Response

Session 3—**THE RESURRECTION**   69
The First Easter Day
The Significance of the Resurrection

THE CONVERSATION   77

Session 4—**WHO IS THE HOLY SPIRIT?**   81
The Day of Pentecost
The Spirit Today

Session 5—**HARVEST TIME: FRUIT AND GIFTS**   91
The Fruit of the Spirit
The Gifts of the Spirit
Preparing to Receive

Session 6—**TIME FOR MINISTRY**   **102**
Practicalities
Luke 11:1-13; John 7:37-39
The Time of Ministry

Session 7—**GROWING UP**   **111**
Facts and Feelings
Afterwards—Difficulties and Opportunities
Growing as a Christian

Session 8—**BEING CHURCH**   **120**
The Body of Christ
Guidance
The Church Member
After the Course

Session 9—**CELEBRATING TOGETHER**   **131**
Option A: Shared Meal and Eucharist
Option B: Evangelistic 'Party with a Purpose'

APPENDIX: Becoming a Christian—Christian Initiation   **137**
The Hexagon of Faith

INTRODUCTION

The church is on the move. God has been doing exciting and delightful things. Renewal in its various forms has invigorated many and puzzled others. New forms of being church have grown many fascinating and different branches. Phrases like 'Messy Church' and 'Fresh Expressions', 'Missional Church' and 'Church Plant' describe different patterns of church life which are still evolving year by year. It is interesting and constructive to see what is happening and see the vigour and new thinking which are taking place. At the same time there are many thousands of churches which are not that different from what they were fifty years ago. Whether new or old they all have the same need.

From the time of the New Testament the church has always been in danger of being absorbed by the details of its own life and letting the conversion and renewal of the individual fade into the background. Corporate life is good, but at its heart is the individual before her or his God.

Saints Alive! is a course which has helped hundreds of thousands to understand the wonder of what God has done for them in Christ and for them to respond in faith and joy. The basic Trinitarian theology behind the course can be used anywhere. In short, Saints Alive!

INTRODUCTION

seeks to lead people into a full-orbed experience of Father, Son and Holy Spirit. (This theological outline is available in the Appendix.)

It has been used by people—
- of different denominations and in many countries;
- in institutions such as prisons and schools;
- in traditional churches and in those formed a couple of years ago;
- in churches which would describe themselves as 'renewed in the Spirit' and those where such a label would not be appropriate and where the jargon and culture of 'renewal' would not be appreciated.

Many scores of training courses for leaders of Saints Alive! groups have been held and it is from these thousands of people that we have learned much which we have incorporated into this edition. We have also spoken to many who are engaged in frontline ministry today.

The world has not stood still since Saints Alive! was first written. There have been changes in society and in the church which have profound implications for those who lead Saints Alive! groups.

- Most people know far, far less about the Christian faith than those of previous generations. Many have virtually no knowledge. Nothing can be assumed, and the flexibility for which Saints Alive! is renowned is more important than ever. People are people, not potatoes, and their personal differences must be honoured, their opinions taken into account and their needs addressed.

- This lack of basic knowledge of the faith is often true of people who have come into our fellowships more recently. They may have been coming for some time but have never had the opportunity to get an overview of the faith and the gospel that they need for personal commitment to Christ. From our experience this is particularly true of the new expressions of church, but is by no means confined to them.
- 'You have to start so much further back these days' is a sentence we have heard again and again. Because of this it may be right in some cases for a group or individuals to take a short starter course before joining a Saints Alive! group.
- 'Belonging comes before believing' is still true. Being in the safety of an accepting, trusting and laughing group enables an individual to think new thoughts and experiment with new adventures.
- Research shows that for most people, coming to faith is a gradual dawning of a new day, though for some, like Saul of Tarsus, it is a sudden experience. Leaders of a Saints Alive! group should be ready for anything and rejoice mightily when it happens.
- Whether it is post-modernism or not, people
    - are more dependent upon their feelings than their reason;
    - are uneasy about committing themselves to a way of life;

INTRODUCTION

find it difficult to think of anything as 'true';
and find it hard to accept a logical argument.

This new edition has been completely revised in the light of what we have learned down the years in a changing church and a changing society. We have found that leaders are always asking for help with the 'mechanics' of leading the course and so the explanatory notes have been expanded. We urge you to read the Introduction and Section 1 carefully before launching forth. The Video 'The Message of the Cross', which has been so important in Session 2, has been retained, but all the other Video material is new.

It has been one of the most fulfilling parts of our ministry to see the joy and surprise in person after person as they come to new life in Christ, and begin to take the first steps in ministering to others in the power of the Spirit.

We pray that God will continue to use this course to enable many more to come to love Christ and walk in the Spirit with the joy of the Father.

Felicity Lawson, John Finney

SECTION 1

WHAT IS THE COURSE?

The Aims of the Course

- It is a nurture course designed to equip churches to help people to come to faith and become active Christians within the church and the world.
- Saints Alive! helps people to explore what it means to live the Christian life in the power of the Holy Spirit.
- It offers participants an opportunity to respond to Christ and experience God's power at work in their own lives.

The Structure of the Course

The course consists of nine sessions. It is designed to be used in small groups, but it can be used within the context of one-to-one mentoring and self-learning. There is a **Leader's Manual** and each course member has a **Journal** which contains notes from each session, Chunk Reading, daily Bible readings and space for personal reflection. There is a **Video** to accompany the course.

WHAT IS THE COURSE?

A glance at the **contents** will show that:

- Session 1 looks at the being of God our Father and our need for a relationship with him.
- Sessions 2 and 3 look at the life, death and resurrection of Jesus Christ.
- Sessions 4 and 5 look at the work of the Holy Spirit.
- Session 6 gives an opportunity for course members to respond to what they have learned and experienced of God so far.
- Sessions 7 to 9 look at the life of the Christian disciple and commitment to the local church.

The biblical basis for this Trinitarian approach is outlined in the Appendix. The 'Hexagon of Faith' and the teaching there have been widely used to illustrate the fullness of God's action in the world and how it has been interpreted by different traditions in the church. You are free to borrow it and use it more widely!

Saints Alive! has three essential elements:

1. Teaching

There are teaching outlines and illustrations for each session. These are not meant to be exhaustive, and leaders should offer their own experience and adapt the notes to fit the different needs of each group.

There are references to places on the internet where some of the most common theological and practical questions are discussed.

The course does not pretend that it can convey the whole expanse of Christian teaching in nine weeks, but it provides basic teaching and an opportunity for ministry. It is designed to give those taking part a hunger to explore further into the immense riches of the faith.

2. Ministry

Ministry has been defined as 'one Christian acting in love to another person'. Suggestions as to when it might be appropriate to invite participants to respond to God's ministry to them are given throughout the course. There are also hints as to how this might be done, but a reliance on the guidance of the Holy Spirit is essential. Opportunities for ministry should be taken whenever it seems right. Participants have the opportunity of a personal conversation (see 'The Conversation', page 77) and the invitation to receive ministry in Session 6 should *always* be made. The usual safeguarding principles regarding pastoral ministry should be strictly adhered to throughout.

3. Fellowship

When people who have been on a nurture course are asked, 'What did you value most?', they often answer, 'Meeting people'. To be in a group where love is shown, confidentialities are kept and they experience the work of God together is a new adventure for most who are there. The chatter before and after sessions is almost as important a part of the course as the more structured times for discussion. Space should be left for this informality, and this may be helped by refreshments.

This 'friendship evangelism' is a very important element as Christ is present in the middle of his followers as they enjoy each other's company.

The Video

The Video contains a mixture of teaching material, testimonies and introductory material to be used at the discretion of the leaders. Timings given below are approximate.

Introduction

    A. Introducing the Course (10 minutes)
    Church and course leaders and members share their experience of Saints Alive! This can be used to introduce the course to decision makers within the local church.

    B. Leading the Course (10 minutes)
    Four people with extensive experience in using Saints Alive! share insights which will help those preparing to lead the course. This material can be found on the website together with other material useful for course leaders (https://saintsalivecourse.com).

    C. The Introductory Meeting (2 minutes)
    Three short clips suitable for showing at the Introductory Meeting.

Session 1—Relationships Matter!

    A. The Two Sons (4 minutes)
A retelling of the parable from Luke 15:11-32.

    B. The Cottage (2 ½ minutes)
A short reflection on Christ's redemptive work in the lives of individuals designed to encourage course members.

Session 2—Who Is Jesus?

    A. Who Is Jesus? (1 minute)
Two short reflections to encourage discussion.

    B. The Message of the Cross (18 ½ minutes)
An illustrated retelling of the Passion.

Session 3—The Resurrection

    A. Mary in the Garden (3 ½ minutes)
Easter morning—Mary's story from John 20:1-18.

    B. The Resurrection Today (3 ½ minutes)
Personal reflections on the Resurrection.

Session 4—Who Is the Holy Spirit?

    The Holy Spirit Today (5 ½ minutes)
Personal experiences of the Holy Spirit.

WHAT IS THE COURSE?

Session 5—Harvest Time: Fruits and Gifts
    A. The Gifts of the Spirit (10 minutes)
    Teaching on the gifts of the Spirit from 1 Corinthians 12.

    B. Experiencing the Gifts (3 ½ minutes)
    Personal experiences of using the gifts.

Session 7—Growing Up (5 minutes)
    Living as a Christian beyond Saints Alive!

Session 8—Being Church (1 minute)
    The impact of a loving church on one individual.

SECTION 2

HOW TO RUN THE COURSE

How Can the Course Be Used?

- As a one-off with church members, to see if it is right for your church.
- As a regular part of the church programme—perhaps being run at the same time as the local school term.
- Continuously, using the witness of one group to gather the next. (Suggestions for this are made at the end of Session 9.)
- With one or two in a discipling/spiritual guidance relationship.

Where Do the People Come From?

Saints Alive! is for those who mean business! It is for anyone who wants to find out more about God's power and love —and who is prepared to do something about it. No Christian knowledge is necessary—just a willingness to discover new treasures.

HOW TO RUN THE COURSE

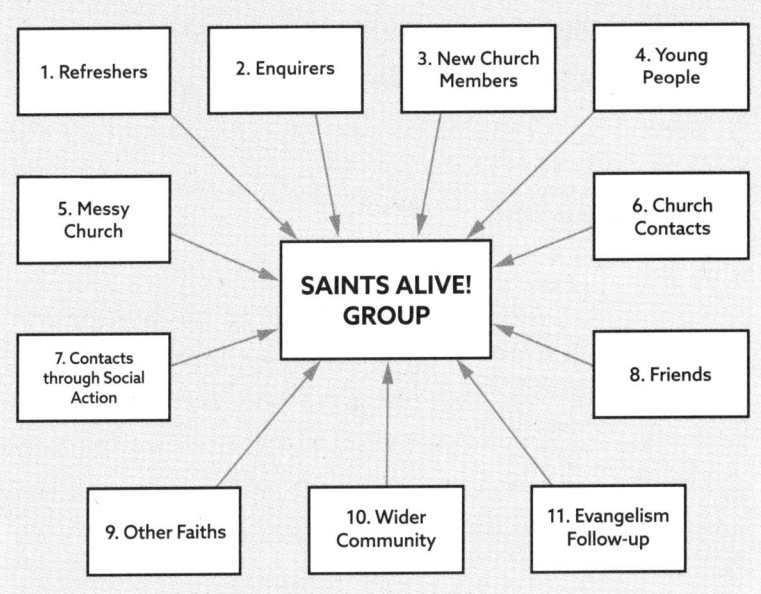

1. Refreshers. We all move from one phase of life to another. As we change, we need to look afresh in a connected way at the story of salvation in the Bible. How does it apply to our lives now? Someone has suggested that 'church members need to go back to basics once every ten years'. All church members have questions which they have wanted to ask for years but have been too shy to ask. Saints Alive! helps people to think and discuss and pray. (Do not skip material because you think it is too 'elementary' for such people: many have never had the chance to piece together the whole wonderful rainbow of God's action.)

2. Enquirers. Some people wander into the orbit of the fellowship and are moved by the Holy Spirit to become hungry to find out more:

'What makes you people tick?' Others are seeking a meaning in life or a purpose in living. Others are curious to find out more about God—even if they do not believe in God.

3. *New church members.* People move into the fellowship from other areas. They need to get to know the heart of the church and meet some of the leaders. If they feel lonely they will also meet some nice people!

4. *Young people*. People as young as fifteen have been through Saints Alive! and had the direction of their lives changed. The course gives them a chance to think through their faith and commit themselves wholeheartedly to God. Some churches have adapted Saints Alive! for use with eleven- to fifteen-year-olds.

5. *Messy Church, etc*. Adults and young people who come to 'alternative services'. 'I came with my daughter and got interested myself ...'

6. *Contacts.* All of us have friends, neighbours and people we meet at the shops. Some churches will have thousands of people who are coming to them asking for funerals and weddings or to use the church premises, etc.

7. *Social action.* Saints Alive! groups have been formed at food banks and similar social enterprises. Why not start a little fellowship to help people with both their physical and spiritual needs? Meet where they usually come and plant a baby church.

Publicity leaflets and invitations for the congregation and other people should set out the purpose of the course and details of the meetings. These should be made freely available in venues other than the church such as the local library, coffee shops and other places where people gather. Members of the congregation should be encouraged to invite their friends.

8. *Friends.* Research shows that people respond best if someone says, 'Would you like to come along with me to …?' This is sometimes called the 'sponsor principle' and can help both the inviter and the invitee grow spiritually.

9. *Other faiths.* Members of other faiths often report unusual dreams, strange compulsions or an overwhelming spiritual hunger which draws them towards Christ. Often they make tentative contact with a Christian group or wander into a church building. They can be spiritually more aware and receptive than others. Welcome them with joy without criticising their former faith or their way of life.

10. *Wider community.* After prayer, one church visited about sixty homes where they felt God had sent them. They asked, 'Would you like to join a group down the road to find out what it is like to be a Christian in X today?' Thirty-eight people joined a group.

11. *Evangelism follow-up.* After an evangelistic effort, Saints Alive! is an ideal course to help those interested to explore further. It includes both teaching and the opportunity to ask questions.

Above all, pray that the right people may come on the course—and the wrong people be kept away! If this is prayed in faith, it means that only the 'right' people will come. We believe God intends to touch every individual who comes—so you can expect them to change!

Where Should It Be Held?

1. Someone's home is often the best option depending on the social context, providing it is large enough for everyone to be seated comfortably.

2. Church premises can work well if there is a comfortable lounge or meeting space.

3. If the group is aimed primarily at those who come to some particular social enterprise or outreach, such as a food bank or a toddler group, then perhaps that venue could be used.

4. Saints Alive! groups have been successfully run in schools, prisons, residential homes and other types of institutions. In prisons it can be part of the 'educational provision'. Where necessary, it can be adapted for those with special needs.

5. Social venues such as pubs, clubs and cafés where others can 'listen in' and chat afterwards with people in the group they know can work well. Those who listen in may actually join the next course.

The Voice of Experience

A) It is common for the first course or two to be fairly large and composed mainly of church members. As confidence in Saints Alive! grows, church members are usually willing to ask their non-Christian friends to come. Later courses often show a drop in numbers but a rise in evangelistic effectiveness.

B) It has been found that it is better for course members to 'opt-in' to the group, rather than Saints Alive! being part of the normal programme for an existing group. Hence it is not always appropriate for a house group or cell church unless all the members really want to grow closer to God.

C) About ten members, including the leaders, in the group is an ideal size. Where a group is larger, there should be an opportunity for smaller groups to be formed from time to time so that the inarticulate can talk, the retiring become known and the burning questions be voiced.

Who Are These People?

Before the course begins, think about and pray for each member.

Ponder these questions about each person:

1. *What is their Christian background—if any?*
Even long-standing church members may have some very strange ideas and may ask some very basic questions.

2. *Why did they join the course?*
You will find out their conscious needs as you meet together, but pray that you may discern their real reasons.

3. *Do they know the Jesus story?*
Many people know nothing about Jesus. Even church members may have a very disjointed and unbalanced view. This course gives an overall view of the life, death and resurrection of Jesus Christ. It is best to assume nothing—the story of the crucifixion may well be new to some: what a wonderful privilege to be telling it to them for the first time!

4. *Have they got a Bible and can they use it?*
It is best if all the group have the same version of the Bible so that they can read together easily. This course uses the New Living Translation. The YouVersion app (or download from www.bible.com) is particularly helpful if a digital version is used. It will be important to make sure that all of them have the necessary 'machinery', know how to find the site and how to navigate it. There are bound to be some technophobes!

Some may never have handled a Bible and will need to be shown the difference between the Old and New Testaments, where the index is and how to find chapter and verse. (An explanation of how to do this is included in the Introduction to the Journal.)

5. *What is their educational background?*
Remember as you begin to plan a session:
- Over 50 percent of the population never read a book, and certainly not one as closely printed as a Bible.

- In a visual age, most people are not used to listening to lectures. Use plenty of visual aids and personal testimony. However, remember that you yourself are the best visual aid: be thrilled by what you are saying and it will communicate.
- Most people have not had a tertiary education.
- We live in the person-centred age of post-modernism, not the modernist age of ideas and words. We need to use pictures, diagrams and, above all, stories. (In the Journal p. 11, participants are encouraged to use sketches, doodles, etc., if they are happier with non-verbal means of expression.)
- Some may be functionally illiterate—being asked to read aloud can be excruciating.

You will often have to move at the speed of the slowest ship in the convoy.

Blessed is the group with a member who is of such simplicity of soul that they ask the questions which everyone else is wanting to ask but dare not!

6. Do they have special needs?

Does anyone have particular needs in terms of access, hearing, vision, food allergies or special diets? This can be checked out at the Introductory Meeting.

Approach and Atmosphere

The atmosphere to communicate during the course is one of 'happy determination'. The mental picture should be of a friendly group of people going on a voyage of discovery—with a seriousness of purpose but a lot of laughter and companionship on the way. Saints Alive! is a course which expects God to be at work in all who are on the course—both the leaders and the members. All are discovering new ways of thinking about God and his world as well as having a fresh encounter with themselves.

If God is at work it does not all depend on us. Deep knowledge of the Bible is useful but far from essential.

Leaders need to know the content of the course well so that they can teach flexibly without constant reference to this Manual. They ought also to have read the Introduction to the Journal and know its structure so that they can guide and encourage its use.

The Voice of Experience

The 4-minute rule—Leaders who are a bit nervous tend to talk too much. It is a useful rule of thumb that if you have spoken uninterruptedly for four minutes it is long enough! It is time to ask a question, invite comments or introduce a visual aid. It is for this reason that the few longer pieces of teaching are on the Video—'The Two Sons', 'The Cottage', 'The Message of the Cross', 'Mary Magdalene' and 'Spiritual Gifts'. These provide a different teaching method and a change of voice.

Flexibility

Saints Alive! is there to be your servant. Change it, adapt it, make it your own. Many leaders find that after leading it a few times, they hardly need to look at the book.

It is flexible enough to be used with different sorts of groups in a variety of settings. Leaders need to adapt it to their own unique situation. It has been used in prisons and in universities, and on every continent except Antarctica. It has been used in groups where no one apart from the leader was a Christian and also in groups where all were ordained ministers.

The Voice of Experience

1. It is generally unwise to lengthen the course by putting in extra sessions or making one session cover more than one meeting (unless a group is still full of questions and asks for more time). Occasional breaks are inevitable, but when spread over too long a time it loses pace. Participants cannot hold in their memory all that has been taught and too much time is spent on recap. A course has a certain 'pace' and if it is too drawn out it loses momentum.

2. For the same reason it is best if there is not more than one session a week. Participants need time to digest and reflect upon each session and the Journal is written with this in mind.

> 3. Whatever pattern of meetings is chosen, the opportunity for ministry in Session 6 should not be missed. It puts into practice what is taught in the course—we need to let God minister to us. To avoid it is to sell the participants short.

Where to Meet

The place the group meets has a big influence on the group. The relaxed atmosphere of a home is preferable to a draughty church hall. Frequently the home of one of the leaders can be used—though they should not be responsible for serving refreshments. A home of one of the group can be used provided they do not feel they have to provide elaborate refreshments. A television and laptop or DVD player will be needed for some sessions.

Food

Research has found that Christian friendship and fellowship have been very important factors in people coming to faith. Refreshments have a part in this, either before or after the sessions. They help people to relax and can be a time for good humour and discovery which lays the foundation for the vital friendships upon which so much depends.

Go with the flow. In most social contexts the simpler and the more informal the better.

HOW TO RUN THE COURSE

However, there are considerable drawbacks if a meal is provided frequently:

- Facilities may be limited and there may not be people to prepare it (who should not be course leaders).
- It can cause domestic friction for course members—a seething wife left at home to put the children to bed is not going to hear the gospel her husband shares with her when he comes home (and even less if he describes the lovely food he has eaten!).
- Meals together may not be part of the normal social context. If houses are small, sumptuous refreshments are not easy.
- The provision of food can be a distraction from the main purpose of the session and can interrupt the informal conversations which can be so important.
- Providing food for course after course can be expensive and demanding for a church.

The Voice of Experience

Different Saints Alive! groups have had varying experiences and there are no general rules. A meal is nearly always valuable as part of Session 9, but generally tea/coffee/biscuits at the beginning and/or end of other sessions has been found to be all that is required to help people to relax and get to know each other.

Visual Aids

Some visual aids can be prepared beforehand, but generally it is best if a picture is built up while the teaching is being given. It is better to draw, however badly, while you talk, than to have it produced neatly in advance. Sometimes an outline can be pencilled in beforehand and then filled in as you talk. Generally it is preferable to draw on a piece of paper attached to a clipboard or on wallpaper/flipchart paper spread on the floor. Avoid standing by the wall in true 'teacher' style, and make sure you are using thick pens and bright colours that can be seen easily by everyone.

We live in a visual age but can become obsessed by over-elaborate visual aids. You are the best visual aid. Enthusiasm communicates.

Worship

Much depends on the people in the group—those with little experience of church life may find prayer awkward and singing unfamiliar songs agonising. Our task is to help people to relax and feel comfortable, not to make them feel embarrassed. Worship should flow from the familiar to the unfamiliar.

Each session should normally begin with prayer, though it may be found that discussion has already begun as people are gathering and the session has already started.

Closing worship should be relaxed. Sing if you have the resources and group members are familiar with the songs—but beware of a Christian sing-along. Members of the group should be invited to participate as soon as they feel comfortable and able to by suggesting topics for prayer, one-sentence thanksgivings or prayers written before the meeting. One-word prayers can help people to get used to the sound of their own voice (e.g., 'Let us pray for those who are ill ... Mary ... Jack ... etc.'). Hopefully with time, participants will grow in confidence and offer their own prayers.

The leaders should pray that as the course continues some of the gifts of the Spirit may be exercised, but this should not be forced. When spiritual gifts are used, the leaders should explain what is happening and be seen to be in control of proceedings. Above all, the prayer time should be kept simple and open to the Holy Spirit.

After the Course

People are never the same after they have been through a Saints Alive! course. Now they need to be integrated into the wider fellowship and encouraged to go on growing and serving as Christians. Careful thought needs to be given to this *before* a course begins—it is too important to leave it to the end.

If a church has a house-group or cell church structure, then it is possible either:

- to feed people from the course into different existing groups; or
- to keep the group together.

In practice the latter has been found to be the most successful if it is at all possible. Most groups develop their own very marked identity and form a network of trusting and caring relationships.

Members do not find it easy to transfer from the 'relaxed warmth' of a group they know and among whom they have found Christ to a group of 'threatening strangers'—however welcoming they are!

If it is decided that the course might continue as a group, then co-leaders, who will become the leaders of the new group, should be included from the start so that they can build relationships with course members.

If the church does not have small groups, then it is important that mature Christians are encouraged to befriend particular course members. After the course is over, these should exercise pastoral oversight and accompany former course members to meetings, etc. These 'sponsors' should not be the leaders of the Saints Alive! group because they cannot provide friendship and care to an ever-increasing number of people.

Above all, it is pastorally disastrous if those who have found Christ through a Saints Alive! group are left unprayed for and uncared for to flounder in the (icy) waters of the church swimming pool.

SECTION 3

THE LEADERS

In every area of church life leadership is vital. Good leadership which takes full advantage of the in-built flexibility of the course will help participants to receive the maximum benefit and grow spiritually.

Leaders of Saints Alive! groups should be mature. This does not mean old leaders but leaders with spiritual understanding and wisdom.

- The notes for each session require leaders to have a certain amount of biblical and spiritual understanding. The course encourages participation by everybody, and leaders have to be prepared to explain Christian truth in a way which provokes discussion. They should not be frightened of the unexpected question and should be able to pick up the insight of others.
- Leaders are not expected to know everything! To say, 'I don't know but I know somewhere that does' is fine. The internet is a wonderful place to turn to for answers. Enter the question in your preferred search engine, and see the answers that emerge. As with all

internet searches, you have to be discerning about the sources of the answers, but there will be something somewhere.

- Leaders should seek to love each one of the group. This makes spiritual demands upon them, for they need to minister deeply at a very important time in the lives of other people.
- The leaders need to be able to give their own testimony to their Christian life—both the joys and the difficulties. This is not a course about the theory of the Christian life but about living it in the power of the Holy Spirit. We cannot lead people where we have not been ourselves. Remember that before Week 6 leaders have to visit and then minister to those in the group individually ('The Conversation', page 77).
- A course like this means teaching adults, and being responsive to the differing needs of each group. (Professional schoolteachers may need to adjust their methods!) Leadership does not require a degree in educational theory, but each session needs decisions on how material is to be presented, what else will be required, how visual aids are to be best used, etc.
- Leaders should be praying that each person taking the course will change: this will make participants very vulnerable as they come under the work of the Holy Spirit. They may go through times of confusion as they find their previous ideas and prejudices challenged and changed. This requires sensitivity and care on the part

of the leaders: they need to be aware of what God is doing in each person and respond appropriately. Leadership is an expression of love.

Training and Supporting Leaders

Leaders should be encouraged to receive training wherever possible. It has been found that the best training is 'on the job'—acting as an assistant leader to experienced leaders who have already been used by God in this ministry. Books and courses on Christian adult education will also be helpful. Saints Alive! groups might spearhead the evangelism of the church and they should receive as much help (and money if necessary) as possible.

> In the Bible, leadership is linked with diligence ... 'If God has given you leadership ability, take the responsibility seriously' (Romans 12:8).

However, we 'do not use words that come from human wisdom. Instead, we speak words given to us by the Spirit' (1 Corinthians 2:13). While training in education and counselling is valuable, the success of a course will come from our ability to hear the voice of the Spirit, and to allow him to speak through us to those on the course. Prayer for all and everything is vital.

The leadership of a Saints Alive! course requires a high degree of commitment, is taxing spiritually and demands much time. It is much more exacting than running a house group. If leaders are doing this regularly with different groups, it is important that the church relieves them of other work in the church. It is important that church members know that a group is meeting and they need to give support by continuing public prayer and encouragement.

Number of Leaders

If possible, we strongly advise that at least two leaders take each group. This biblical model of Christian leadership provides mutual support and differences of style and of teaching gifts. It also provides a measure of safeguarding and greater availability for pastoral care of group members.

If you expect that the course will continue as a group, then assistant leaders need to be included from the beginning. They can be introduced as such at the first meeting and included, as appropriate, in the planning, teaching and any time of ministry. If the group is larger than about fifteen people, then it will be helpful to appoint assistant leaders who will be able to lead small discussion groups and so on.

The Voice of Experience

Churches running these courses have found that it is helpful if someone in senior leadership in the church helps to lead one or two courses when they are first introduced. However, courses are demanding of time and energy and it is often best if they train others to take over the leadership as soon as possible.

Feedback suggests that it is also valuable if the leaders differ from each other—lay/ordained, women/men, younger/older. The course contains direct pastoral ministry in 'The Conversation' with each group member, and the pastoral sensitivity that this needs should also be taken into account.

Using the Video

The Video contains helpful insights and advice from experienced leaders (Introduction, B. Leading the Course). This section of the Video and further comments from course leaders can also be found on the website https://saintsalivecourse.com. Course leaders should familiarise themselves with the Video when planning the course.

SECTION 4

BEFORE YOU START ...

If you are thinking of using Saints Alive! these are some points to think through. It is best not to rush at this stage but quietly and prayerfully help others to get enthusiastic!

CHECKLIST

❏ Read through the introductory sections thoroughly—they should answer many of your questions.

❏ Talk over the proposed course with the leaders of the fellowship—elders, church council, minister, etc. If Saints Alive! is being used for the first time, consider using the relevant parts of the Video and/or invite someone who has used the course to speak from their experience. Ensure a church leader is available for the Introductory Meeting or Party—this is a course for the whole church to pray about and support.

❏ Arrange a meeting for the course leaders before the Introductory Meeting. Go through the course in outline together so that you all gain an overview. It would be helpful to watch the Video and see how the elements within it can be used. 'Pray in' the course members.

BEFORE YOU START ...

- ❏ Pencil in where and when the course will meet. Be flexible about this until the Introductory Meeting when course members can discuss what would suit them best.

- ❏ Decide what will happen when the course ends. If you want the group to continue as a group, it is a help if you discern who might be assistant leaders who can take part in the course.

- ❏ Publicise the Introductory Meeting/Party (see pp. 39-44). Begin prayerfully to suggest to potential participants that they might like to think about joining the course. Publicity should be widespread so that anyone is free to join, and there is no suspicion of an exclusive 'hole-in-the-corner' group being formed.

- ❏ There should be some ways in which prospective members can show their interest—a sheet of paper to sign up in church, reply forms on publicity, email/text responses, etc. This helps to begin the process of commitment and gives you some idea of the numbers involved. Often it is best if people are invited just to the Introductory Meeting/Party so they can hear what is on offer and then make a decision.

- ❏ Purchase sufficient copies of the Journal. Decide if you will give them to course members or if you will encourage them to buy them. Sometimes people value most what they have bought themselves.

- ❏ Purchase the course Video and ensure there is a screen and laptop available when you will need them.

❏ Put dates in diaries for preparation meetings between the sessions.

❏ Decide what version of the Bible you want to use—it is a great help if the group are using the same edition with the same page numbers. We have found the New Living Translation particularly useful for those with little Christian background, and the course and the Journal have been based on it. The course asks members to read fairly long passages from the Bible so a modern version is helpful. Some course members may prefer to use a digital version rather than a paper one. You will need to decide:

> a) whether Bibles are to be loaned or given to participants, or
> b) they should be encouraged to buy copies (which should be available for purchase at the Introductory Meeting), or
> c) all the group will use a digital version (such as the YouVersion app) throughout.

If the group has people who are non-literate or functionally illiterate, they can be guided to CDs or appropriate websites of Mark's gospel, Acts and Philippians. The YouVersion app has an audio facility which will be found helpful for the Chunk Readings.

❏ If food is being provided, decide how this is going to happen—and who will be responsible. (See more on the pros and cons of food on pages 26-27.)

INTRODUCTORY MEETING OR PARTY

(A more eye-catching title is often used: e.g., 'Let's get started!', or something biblical, like, 'Come and see'.)

There are different ways in which this can take place and different places which are most appropriate.

1. A fairly business-like meeting may take only 30-45 minutes, perhaps after a service or regular gathering. It may be more convenient to hold it on church premises. Provide refreshments to encourage chatter and banish shyness. A little light banter is to be encouraged, as those from outside the church may expect long faces and solemnity.

2. Alternatively, you can have a party and invite people to come. It can be somewhere with no church connotations or on church premises. In some social settings you can have a sit-down meal, while in

others a buffet with light refreshments may be more appropriate. The local pub may be able to provide both premises and food. Church members should only come with someone new—and they can then be encouraged to come to at least the first session of the course if the person they bring decides to join. As in all open gatherings, care should be taken with regard to potential safeguarding issues.

Someone from the church leadership should introduce the group leaders.

If it is decided to show 'The Introductory Meeting' from the **Video**, the arrangements should be made beforehand along with decisions about at what point in the meeting it is to be shown.

Administrative arrangements should be carefully prepared—it shows that the course leaders are efficient and sensible. Uncertainty increases nervousness.

- This meeting is essential, and prospective members should be encouraged to make every effort to attend. It helps to set the 'tone' of the course. The mental picture to communicate is that it will be relaxed but purposeful … with a lot of laughter and camaraderie. They will be part of a friendly group of people going on a voyage of discovery—there is seriousness of purpose but a lot of fun on the way.
- Prior to the meeting you will need to decide (a) whether the Journal is to be given to or purchased

INTRODUCTORY MEETING OR PARTY 41

by participants and (b) whether NLT Bibles are to be available for borrowing/purchase. (Alternatively, you can simply direct people to the free YouVersion app.)

You will need to make the following points at some juncture:

- Joining the course is an important undertaking, and it demands commitment in setting aside time to attend and to use the Journal.
- Regular attendance is expected. If you want to drop out at any time, that is fine (though it would be helpful if you let us know or we shall think you are ill!).
- We have copies of the Journal available for you to purchase now and they will also be available on the first week of the course. OR: We have copies of the Journal to give you, so don't forget to collect one when you sign up.
- We shall be using the New Living Translation of the Bible either as a book or as an app, and books will be available at the first meeting for those who want them.

The Voice of Experience says that it is much better to set a fairly high bar in what is expected of participants regarding attendance, completing the Journal, etc. If it is set low ('Come when you can', 'Do the Journal when you feel like it'), it suggests that finding out about the Christian faith is not very important and that God is just a passing interest of no more significance than a course on growing tomatoes.

What Is the Course Like?

You might like to say the following:

- The course is for beginners, not experts. We won't make any assumptions about what you know. We will be starting at the beginning, and we do not shock easily! Anything you don't know or any questions about the existence of God, etc., are fine.
- It is a nine-session course, during which we shall look at the work of God the Father and how he sent his Son, Jesus, and the Holy Spirit into our world.
- However, we shall not only be looking backwards at what happened two thousand years ago, but at what those events mean to us today. We shall be seeing again and again how these can make a difference in our everyday lives. We shall also be looking for God to touch each of our lives in different ways and there will be times when we can open ourselves to him if we wish.
- The course will mean different things to each person, because we all come with different needs and from different backgrounds. Some will know quite a lot about God. Others know virtually nothing. For some the Bible is a familiar friend, for others a closed book. It does not matter, for we are expecting everyone to come closer to Christ and to discover more of his will for their lives. And that is true of the leaders—we also will learn and change!

INTRODUCTORY MEETING OR PARTY

- Course members usually get to know each other quite well during a course, and this is one of its perks. However, it is quite all right to come along and say nothing. *[Do not worry—it is very unlikely that they will stay silent for very long, but some may be very apprehensive of what might be demanded of them in terms of participation.]*
- All discussion is helpful and there will be lots of opportunities to ask questions, but argument for argument's sake will harm the group.
- To make for free discussion it is expected that members will keep confidential anything they learn in the group about other people—but anything they learn about the Christian faith they can talk about with anyone! *[They may need reminding about confidentiality at other times during the course—and the leaders should set an example!]*

Practicalities

- Each session is like a football match: it will last for ninety minutes, though if the group wants to go on to extra time, that will only be for half an hour. There will always be a break at ninety minutes for those who are being picked up or catching a bus. It has been found that texts at the end of meetings are a very good way of asking for pick-ups.
- Is there anyone who does not have easy access to the internet? This is not essential—but useful. If you are

on the internet, it would be helpful if you could let us have your email addresses. *[Pass round a board with paper and pen.]*

- If anyone wants to get in touch with us, our email address is here. *[Hand round paper.]*
- Please bring your Journal (and Bible) to sessions. Nobody will want to see the Journal—it is private: just for you to make notes in/draw pictures in/doodle if you wish.
- Does anyone have particular needs in terms of access, hearing, vision, seating, allergies or special diets? Please let us know before you leave so we can be ready to welcome you and make you as comfortable as possible.
- Arrange the date, place and time of at least the first three sessions. Suggest that members might like to help each other with transport. *[This begins to build relationships and also helps those who will find getting to the first session a nerve-wracking business, especially if it is held in a big house.]*
- Don't worry if you can't remember everything: a written reminder/email of the times and places decided at this Introductory Meeting will be sent round before the first meeting.
- Please begin to pray for each other—and for the leaders.
- You are not the only person feeling nervous/excited! Does anyone have any questions?

Session 1

RELATIONSHIPS MATTER!

———

Aims:

- To meet each other.
- To put everyone at ease.
- To think about relationships—with each other and with God.

LEADING THE SESSION

In this session, establishing healthy dynamics within the group is really important from the outset. A light but firm touch is required from the leaders.

If there are a lot of people from the fringes or from right outside the church, they may need to be reassured that they are not the only ones who:

- Are feeling nervous and worried that they will be put into toe-curlingly embarrassing situations.
- Are not sure what they think about God or church or the Bible.

The content is intended to be straightforward enough to enable non-Christians to have as much to offer as those who have been Christians for years. Everyone can speak about their experience of life and relationships. At the same time, no one should be put in the position where they are forced to speak. Fear of making a fool of oneself may be very near the surface.

In this session, although we retell the story of the two sons, it is best not to ask group members to open their Bibles until the very end when talking about the Journal. Remember that some of them may be very unfamiliar with handling any book, let alone one as big and complicated as the Bible.

An introductory ice-breaker may be used but is not essential.

Decide before the session whether you are going to use 'The Two Sons' and/or 'The Cottage' from the **Video**.

Refreshments

People relax if their hands are occupied. Tea or coffee and a biscuit will always help. (See Section 2 on the pros and cons of more elaborate food.) Much depends on the social norms of the people in the group—elaborate meals may make some feel awkward while others may come straight from work and need something more substantial.

Leaders should be introducing people to each other rather than working in the kitchen!

PRESENTATION

In this manual, teaching material is in 'normal' print and notes for your guidance are in italics.

Prayer

A brief prayer may set the tone for the course, but often the introductions flow naturally from the refreshments and it is best to allow that to happen.

Introductions

The relationships between members of the group are very important. Even more important is the way in which the leaders are regarded—as a schoolteacher? ... friend? ... senior? ... expert? ... companion on the Way? Leaders should not give the impression that they know the answer to everything. Avoid going round the group asking each person to say something about themselves—it can be terrifying for some people.

It may be helpful to use some sort of ice-breaker, but it should not take too long. If the group mixes well, it may be unnecessary, though a good ice-breaker enables even groups who know one another to discover new things. If leaders expect group members to be open with them, then they themselves should be vulnerable. One simple ice-breaker is to ask people to tell the group, or in a pair, how they got their name. Our names are about our identity. It is also helpful to group leaders to get people's name clearly in their minds from the outset.

Leaders should introduce themselves by giving a few facts about themselves, but it is not a time for a C.V. or a testimony. Avoid facts which some group members cannot relate to (e.g. a degree when some of the group have left school as soon as they could).

Expectations

Has anyone any expectations or feelings as the course begins? [*No one is obliged to speak.*]

This can set some boundaries—e.g., this is not a complete course on Christian theology or ethics—nor does it tussle with current political or international issues. It is a basics course to help us to explore the Christian faith, either for the first time or as a refresher. It may be important to remind folk what was said at the Introductory Meeting—e.g., no question is too basic or silly. The group will be discussing the Christian faith in a setting which is comfortable and confidential.

Human Relationships

We all have something in common which can bring the most joy or sometimes the most misery into our lives. What is it? *Answer: relationships.*

RELATIONSHIPS MATTER!

We all have a network of relationships, some with people we are close to and others with those we don't know so well. What relationships can you suggest?

Draw a sample relationship map on a big piece of paper (wallpaper is good). Put an imaginary person at the centre and draw all the relationships they might have. This is best done by one of the leaders kneeling on the floor and writing the answers that group members give.

Note that the quality of relationships may vary—not least within families. Some sisters and brothers do not get on! Work relationships may be supportive or destructive. Some relationships will be deeper or more superficial than others.

Time also matters. Lovers do not always love forever.
On another piece of paper put the personal effects of relationships.

When relationships are positive, how does it make us feel? *Take suggestions from the group but be ready to start the ball rolling.*

Members may suggest:
- feeling good about ourselves
- valued/supported
- able to grow
- more ready to launch out

When relationships are poor we may feel: *Again take suggestions from the group.*
- without worth/unloved
- angry

anxious/bitter
unable to reach our full potential

Relationships can end when:
there is an almighty quarrel with anger and slammed doors
people drift apart without realising it
other relationships take priority
people develop different interests
people have different aims and priorities
people get bored with each other

Relationship with God

The Bible and Christian experience down the centuries tell us that, amazing as it may seem, God wants a relationship with us. God created us and loves us. Totally, unconditionally. Loving relationships are at the very heart of God, whom Christians know as Father, Son and Holy Spirit. *(Don't get mired in a discussion about the nature of the Trinity at this point!)*

Jesus prayed to God as Father. Not everyone has a good relationship with their parents, but we all know what is involved in good parenting. What does an ideal parent give? *Suggestions from group:*
appropriate care as we grow up
stability
food and warmth

love/acceptance
freedom to be ourselves

The other side to this is what we think an ideal child should give to their parents: *Again suggestions from group:*
love
helpfulness
trust

If children are unsure of the love of a parent, they may try to 'buy' their love by such things as:
slaving round the house
over-working at school/striving to achieve
being strangely well-behaved

or they may:
rebel against their parents
have temper tantrums
go their own way
be disobedient

Neither is good. The first leads to a worried, over-conscientious person and the second to an adult who finds it difficult to trust others or make deep relationships.

Often a poor relationship with our parents—or indeed anyone who is in authority—can be one of the factors which influences the way we see God.

What Do People Think of God?

*Not necessarily how **we** think about God, which may be too personal at this point, but how do people in general think about God? Do not assume that your concept of God is the same as group members'.* **Don't be critical of views expressed at this stage.**

Some people may see 'God' as:
- identified with nature
- a benevolent old-man-in-the-sky
- an autocrat who makes demands—a policeman or head teacher who keeps accounts of wrongs
- one among many—as in some polytheistic religions
- a generalised force for good
- an impersonal spirit—as in much New Age thinking
- something out there which has influence over my life—through the stars, crystals, extra-terrestrials, hexing, etc.
- non-existent
- a figment of people's imagination—for those who need a prop in life

The Bible speaks of God as a person who wants a relationship with human beings and is continually reaching out to them in love. Christians believe that Jesus shows us what God is like, but we shall be thinking a bit more about that next week.

God the Father has all that we look for in an ideal parent and much, much more.

But we can behave like children trying to earn their parents' favour by giving presents to our heavenly Father: *A sheet of paper should be pre-prepared with the outline of various 'presents' sketched in: write suggestions inside the outlines. There may be suggestions like, being good … going to church …. obeying 'rules'.*

Our capacity to want to do our own thing means our relationship with God can break down in very similar ways to human relationships breaking down.

Although we are talking about 'sin' it may not be helpful to use that word at this point unless all the group already have some Christian background. So many people think of sin as doing bad things rather than being about our attitude towards God.

> *Ask the group why our relationship with God might break down.*

- perhaps we have never had a relationship with God because of our upbringing
- anger and rejection following an episode where we feel God has let us down or wasn't there when we needed him
- drifting apart from God without realising it
- other relationships become more important—Christian fellowship takes second place
- we develop different interests—the church no longer has any attraction for us
- we choose different values—in defiance of God
- boredom with God—there seems no spice in living as a Christian
- believing in God is no longer 'cool'—as for many teenagers
- life becomes busy—demanding job/young family, etc.

It might be best to leave this hanging at this point unless group members start identifying with particular reasons for a less-than-perfect relationship with God. If this happens, acknowledge their contribution and thank them for sharing.

One well-known story Jesus told speaks about God's longing to have a relationship with us.

*Either show the **Video** of the 'Session 1, A. The Two Sons' (Luke 15:11-32) or retell it in your own words.*

If there is time, encourage a general discussion on the story. You may find one or two of these questions helpful to begin:

1. Who do you identify with—father/younger brother/older brother? Why?
2. If we identify the father with God the Father, what does that tell us about God and his longing for a relationship with us?
3. Has there ever been a time when you 'came to your senses' and started to change your life around?
4. St Augustine said, 'You have made us for yourself and our hearts are restless until they find their rest in you.' Have you ever known that sense of restlessness, of searching for something or someone even if you don't know what/who it is?
5. The father accepted both of the brothers because they were part of his family, whatever they had, or had not, done. The Bible talks of God's love being completely certain and absolutely nothing can destroy it. Someone once said, 'God can never love you more

than he does at this moment and he can never love you less.'

Loving and Being Loved

Loving relationships make an impact on our lives. Think of falling in love with someone. Andrew Lloyd Webber's song 'Love Changes Everything' encapsulates this.

Some change happens naturally. When people fall in love, those around them notice the change. Knowing you are loved makes you feel better about yourself. You want to do things to show your love for the other person. You think about what the other person feels or needs. But as the relationship grows, some changes have to be worked at because none of us is perfect and the broken or damaged parts of our lives can annoy or hurt the other person. It may be as silly as who puts the rubbish out at night! In a truly loving relationship people grow and fulfil more of their potential.

Jesus said, 'My purpose is to give [you] a rich and satisfying life' (John 10:10). Because God loves us he wants us to be more and more the people he created us to be.

Our prayer is that during the course each of us will grow in our relationship with God, whether we have been a Christian for years or whether at this point we are not even sure that God exists. He will work in each one of us differently because each one of us is unique. Each of us is at a different stage of our lives and our Christian journey.

For each of us this will mean change. Change is not something we need to be frightened about, for this is change for the better. Change is part of life and what doesn't change is dead. If you are alive you change!

We finish our session with a short time when we can be still and meditate—you can close your eyes if you want:

*The verbal picture below is on the **Video** 'Session 1, B. The Cottage' or can be used by one of the leaders to draw together what has been said.*

Think of a beautiful cottage that has become derelict. The garden is overgrown, the floorboards are rotten, there are holes in the roof *(pause to let the group visualise the cottage)*. It was designed to be perfect—a thing of beauty and an ideal home, but now it is broken down and in need of thorough restoration.

Someone comes along who sees the cottage, knows how it was meant to be and buys it. He then sets about restoring it to its former glory. Unlike most of us, he is not an enthusiastic amateur but an experienced expert who knows exactly what he is doing. He sets about his work of restoration in precisely the right way for that particular cottage. Some jobs are obvious and anyone looking at the cottage can see what he is doing. Others are less obvious but nevertheless essential. He does not give up until the work is complete.

(Application)

The Bible says that 'God bought you with a high price' (1 Corinthians 6:20) and in Christ we are being re-created to be like him. God knows us and loves us as individuals, and he sees all our potential. Although sometimes his work in our lives may seem drastic—like taking up the rotten floorboards!—he knows precisely what he is doing, and we can trust him not to do more in our lives at any one time than the structure can take—the house is not going to collapse.

There will be times as Christians when it is obvious what God is doing in our lives and times when, though work is still going on, it will be less obvious. He will not give up on us until his work is complete. Therefore, we need not be frightened of change, because God knows what he is doing.

Neither do we need to be dismayed if at times he seems to be more obviously at work in someone else than he is in us.

Jesus came to show us that the Father's love does not have to be earned but is free—he loves us just as we are, and he longs to forgive us and put right the break in relationships.

More about that next week.

Conclude with a short prayer thanking God that he loves us and wants a relationship with us.

Introduce the Journals

Make sure everyone has got a book. (These should have been given out at the Introductory Meeting but some of the group may have missed this.)

Take them to Week 1 and show them the three sections:
- *An outline of this session and space to make their own notes*
- *Chunk Reading*
- *Daily Bible Readings*

This pattern is followed every week.

Show them the Introduction where there is an explanation of how to find passages in the Bible and different ways to pray. (This is important even for church members, fewer of whom read the Bible at home than you may imagine.)

Explain that during the course we will read Mark's gospel, the Acts of the Apostles and Paul's letter to the Philippians in 'chunks'. This is not as daunting as it sounds as the chunks will never take longer than thirty minutes to read. But some people may prefer to listen to the Chunk Readings on a CD or on the internet. The YouVersion app has an audio function. Encourage them, if they do nothing else this week, to read or listen to Mark chapters 1 to 8 because we shall be talking about what we have read in the next session.

Assure the group that the Journal is for their personal use. No one will ever ask to see it, let alone mark it!

Refreshments

It might be worth offering further refreshments as it gives anyone who wants to an excuse to hang around and talk further or ask questions they daren't ask in the group.

Send them on their way and say you look forward to seeing them next week.

Session 2

WHO IS JESUS?

Aims:

- To help group members come to an understanding of who Jesus is and what he did.
- To challenge them with the personal significance of the cross for each of us.

LEADING THE SESSION

The meeting begins by making the portrait of Christ that members have gained from their Chunk Reading. Make sure you have a good supply of A4 paper available. If you have a small group you might like to add to your picture by watching the brief comments on the **Video** 'Session 1, A. Who Is Jesus?'.

'The Message of the Cross' on the **Video**, despite its restrained handling of the Passion, always has a great impact. It is likely that the group will not want to talk much afterwards, so be prepared to leave a bit of space and then move directly to the response and the diagram of the four circles for which you will need flipchart paper or wallpaper.

During this session group members will be using their Bibles for the first time together. Be aware of those for whom this is a new activity, including many churchgoers who may be used to seeing Bible passages on a notice sheet or screen. Avoid excessive page turning and gently assist those who may be unfamiliar with looking up Bible passages, being sensitive to any feelings of inadequacy.

PRESENTATION

Introduction and Prayer

Welcome members back and ask how people got on with their Journals. Explain that individual questions or problems can be discussed after the session or if they need to leave immediately to catch a bus, etc., perhaps a phone call or conversation later in the week.

Begin with a brief prayer asking that during this session each one of us may grow in our understanding of who Jesus is and what he has done for us.

The Person of Jesus

The Chunk Reading of Mark 1 to 8 asked **'What sort of person is Jesus and what kind of things did he do?'** Ask the group what words we might use to describe him—e.g., compassionate, strong, friendly ...

Spend some time on this, encouraging every member of the group to make a contribution. Write answers with thick, bold-coloured felt tips

WHO IS JESUS? 61

and large lettering on separate pieces of A4 and put them on the floor in the centre of the group. It usually works best if one of the leaders is drawing out the answers and the other acting as scribe.

Spend some time looking together at what has been written. What stands out for the group about the portrait of Jesus they have prepared? You may need to talk about how Jesus could be both loving and at times angry or other characteristics which may appear to conflict with one another.

Notice his humanity as well as the signs of his divinity. Jesus shows us what it means to be truly human as well as showing us what God is like. Because he is fully human, people can identify with him and, very importantly, there is nothing we can go through in life that he cannot understand.

Notice too that Jesus began his public ministry when he was anointed with the Holy Spirit at his baptism. (Mark begins his gospel at this point and doesn't record anything about the birth of Jesus.) *Don't spend long on it at this point, but it is important at this early stage to link Christ's ministry with the coming of the Spirit.*

On the **Video** *there are two short comments by other people about Jesus which may be used at this point.*

Who Is He?

Read Mark 8:27-33 together. The time came when Jesus asked his disciples who other people thought he was. Then he asked them who they thought he was. There comes a point when all of us have to answer that question.

Look at the answers that were given by 'the people'—they are looking at important people from the past. (John the Baptist had recently been beheaded by Herod.) Peter correctly identifies Jesus as the promised Messiah, the one who would set the Jewish people free. But Jesus was not the kind of Messiah the Jews were expecting—a military and political liberator or a supernatural wonder worker. He had rejected these models at his temptations.

But even Peter couldn't understand what Jesus was saying about what it would mean for Jesus to be the Messiah. Jesus' understanding of his calling was shaped by the passages in Isaiah about the Suffering Servant whose path to glory is the way of suffering. And for Jesus, of course, that meant the way of the cross.

There may well be people in the group who are not yet ready to answer that question for themselves, and in many ways they cannot be expected to until they have seen the whole picture.

The Passion

For the rest of this session, the focus is on the last week of Jesus' life—what is often called 'The Passion'. There are lots more things we could look at, but Christians believe the events of this last week are so important that we want to leave plenty of time to reflect on them. *Let the group flick through their Bibles and see the proportion of the Gospels given over to the last week.*

Show 'Session 2, B. The Message of the Cross' from the **Video**. *Explain that even in church we often don't hear how the whole week fits together. The Video is based round still pictures depicting the events of the week with the narrative based on passages from the Gospels. It is longer than most of the Video clips in Saints Alive! because the events* it recalls are so important. Many, even those for whom the story is very familiar, will find the narrative very moving. Pray for a spiritual rather than emotional impact.*

The Importance of Response

Allow the silence which normally follows the showing of 'The Message of the Cross' to last as long as is helpful as group members reflect on what they have seen and heard before moving on to this section. Don't be in too much of a hurry to fill the silence with words if there is a sense of the Spirit really moving. What can seem an age to us may not be that long if the Spirit is at work.

The end of the Video reminds us that there are various responses we can make to the death of Jesus. The one thing we cannot do is nothing—that in itself is rejection, for to ignore someone is to reject them.

The New Testament describes a Christian as someone who is 'in Christ' for whom Jesus is Lord of their lives. To be a Christian is to acknowledge that Jesus died for our sins so that we might be forgiven and put back into a right relationship with God. That is the symbolism of the curtain in the Temple being torn in two. (This curtain separated the Holy of Holies—which symbolised the very presence of God himself—from the rest of the Temple. No one could enter except the High Priest once a year. The death of Jesus opens the way for everyone who wants to have a relationship with God.)

There are different ways in which human beings can relate to God which can be explained using this simple visual aid:

1. *Draw a large circle on paper on the floor and explain that this circle represents our life. In the circle draw a series of smaller circles representing different aspects of our lives, e.g., F = Family, W = Work, R = Relationships and friendships, L = Leisure activities. Put an 'I' in the centre and explain that this circle represents the life without God where 'I' decide what I will do. Put a smaller circle outside the main one and put a + in it.* The cross is outside because Jesus has no place in this life. **This person, however good their life, would not consider themselves a Christian.**

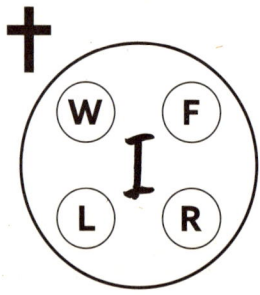

2. *Draw a second circle identical to the first but with a faint dotted cross in it.* This represents the life that used to be strongly Christ-centred but has allowed that faith to become a faint memory of long ago. **This is the nostalgic Christian.** *(Many who come on the course identify with this circle.)*

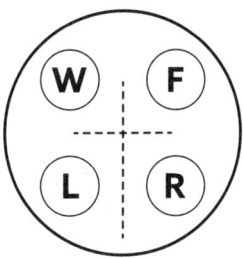

3. Draw another circle identical to the first but containing a small circle with a cross in it. Explain that this represents a life where the Christian faith, praying and even going to church are important but where the individual remains firmly in control. Faith is essentially one interest among many and there may be some areas in the person's life where they do not welcome God or Christian values. **The restricted Christian.**

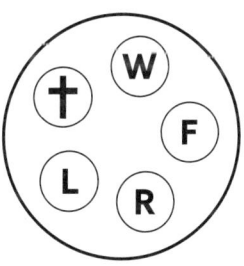

4. Draw a fourth circle where the central 'I' has been replaced by the cross. It is on the cross that Jesus shows us the full extent of his love. It is only as we know ourselves loved totally and unconditionally that we can give ourselves to this amazing God and Jesus is allowed to be the centre of our life. He is our Lord and influences every aspect of our being—our attitude to work, our relationships, our political opinions, how we spend our leisure, etc. This is what Jesus died to achieve, for it is only when he is at the centre of our lives as Lord that we are truly ourselves, truly the people God created us to be. We know that God loves us, really loves us, and this sets us free from having to achieve or do or be anything to get his approval. This is at the heart of what it means to be **a Christian disciple**.

Invite the group to look at the circles and, if they haven't already done so, to think where they best fit in. Don't ask them to share this but welcome comments from anyone who wants to do so.

(This illustration has been particularly helpful to those who would not consider themselves Christians but who have a vague spirituality that is a significant part of their lives. It raises for them the question

'Where does Jesus fit in?' It is also useful for those who have been going to church for years and for whom their faith, in so far as they have understood it, has been important. It does not ask people to deny their past but recognises that we are on a journey which takes us from where we are towards understanding the meaning of fullness of life in Christ.)

Even once we have surrendered our lives to God in Christ, we do not always live fully in circle 4. That's why as Christians we offer our lives afresh to God each day, repent of the things which draw us away from him and ask for his grace to follow Jesus faithfully.

Prayer

Move from a consideration of our response to the love of God in Christ to a time of prayer. In practice it has been found best not to lead in a prayer of commitment at this stage. Participants will have the opportunity for a more considered response in Session 6. By that time they should have a fuller understanding of what they are doing and of the work of the Holy Spirit and will not be pressurised by the emotional impact of the Video or by group expectations. It may, however, be right to lead in a prayer in which each member of the group has the opportunity to dedicate themselves to continuing to seek God, to learn more and to respond to God at the right time.

Depending on the group, it may be right for the leaders to pray or to have an open time of prayer when members can thank God for Jesus. But keep prayers short and without too much religious jargon. That will only stop the less confident from daring to join in!

Journals

The Chunk Reading this week is Mark 8 to 16, which records the events we have been thinking about in this session. The daily readings offer further reflection on the death of Jesus and point us towards next week, where we will be thinking about his resurrection.

Session 3

THE RESURRECTION

Aims:

- To explore the accounts of the resurrection and ascension.
- To explore the significance of the resurrection.
- To introduce members to using the Bible for group study.

LEADING THE SESSION

There is a lot of material to get through in this session. It is important to keep things moving whilst still encouraging maximum participation from group members. Most of the session revolves around a study of Luke 24. Group members should be encouraged to follow the passage in their Bibles. The **Video** of 'Mary in the Garden' helps set the scene.

For the first time this session encourages members to share what God is doing in their lives. This can be a great encouragement to the whole group and should not be rushed.

PRESENTATION

Begin the session with prayer.

Journal

Invite any questions or reflections on last week's Journal. Now that they have had a chance to reflect, what was the impact of the Video outlining the events of the last week of Jesus' life? Give space for sharing about this or about the four circles.

The First Easter Day

*If you are using the **Video** resources, watch the account of Mary Magdalene in the garden and then ask the group what they think the disciples made of her story. They were incredulous!*

Remind the group where we left off last week with the crucifixion and Jesus being placed in the tomb. Explore together how the disciples would have felt.

- shock
- confusion
- disbelief that it had happened
- anger
- numbness
- fear for themselves

Perhaps some within the group have experienced sudden and unexpected bereavement and may share something of their experience. Be

THE RESURRECTION

aware that even if the bereavement happened some time ago, feelings may still be quite raw. Be gentle with them.

Read Luke 24:13-24.

The setting is Easter day. Cleopas and his companion were followers of Jesus but not members of the twelve disciples. They had been in Jerusalem for the Passover, but we don't know whether they witnessed the crucifixion or only heard about it from those who were there. They had clearly been with Jesus' disciples as the events of Easter day unfolded.

As the scripture is read, see what stands out for you—what you notice. *One of the leaders should read the passage and then ask the group what they noticed.* **How were Cleopas and his companion? What was their mood? What were they saying to each other?** Probably many of the emotions we have just been speaking about. They may well have been going over and over the events that had taken place and asking 'Why?'

What impact did the reports of the women and the others who had been to the tomb have on them?

Why didn't they recognise Jesus when he drew alongside them? *Not expecting to see him because they thought he was dead. Too caught up in their own emotions to take on board new information.*

Why did Jesus ask them what they were talking about? *They needed to talk and tell him their story.*

Now read Luke 24:25-32.
What is Jesus doing in verses 25-27? *Giving them a new perspective. Helping them to see that the crucifixion wasn't a terrible mistake.*

Now look at verses 28-29. What strikes you in these verses? Why do you think that Jesus 'acted as if he were going on'? What made the disciples invite him to stay? *Perhaps Jesus made as if he were going on because he was waiting for their invitation? Jesus never forces himself on anyone; he waits until they are ready to take the next step of faith.*

Now consider verses 30-32. What is significant about these verses? *Their eyes were opened—they suddenly saw that it was Jesus. This was a moment of revelation, of spiritual insight. (So far as we know these two disciples were not at the Last Supper, so it was not simply a sparking of memory.)* How had they felt while Jesus had been talking with them on the road?

Sharing

Ask the group whether any of them feel that they have had eye-opening moments either in the past or during the course so far. Can anyone

THE RESURRECTION

identify with the disciples when they say, 'Didn't our hearts burn within us?' Does anyone feel excited by being part of this group and discovering more about God?

Leave plenty of opportunity for sharing. If no one says anything, perhaps one of the group leaders could share how they came to know Jesus, but it is better if the testimonies come from within the group.

It is worth noting that although the events in this passage last part of a day, for many of us the journey to faith takes a lot longer with lots of little eye-opening moments along the way. And it's a journey that never comes to an end because there is always more to know and discover.

Now read Luke 24:33-43.

The reaction of Cleopas and his companion is to rush back to Jerusalem to tell their friends the good news that Jesus is alive. When they get there they discover that the amazing news has got there before them because Jesus has also appeared to Peter.

Explain briefly that the events of the first Easter day are hard to piece together. Each gospel tells the story slightly differently. This is part of their authenticity, reflecting that they are eyewitness accounts with different people remembering different parts depending on their personal involvement and then passing their memories on to those who wrote the Gospels. The gospel writers then selected from those memories the particular aspects of the many different resurrection appearances which fitted best with their particular telling of the story of Jesus.

You may want to point out to the group the summary of the resurrection appearances in the Journal, but don't spend time looking at it in any detail at this point.

Now turn back briefly to Luke 24:36-43 and ask what strikes them in this passage. Note the fear of the disciples who thought they had seen a ghost, despite having just been told that Jesus had appeared to Peter and the two disciples on the road. They are invited to touch his wounds as is Thomas in John 20:27. Jesus eats to prove they are not seeing a ghost.

The Significance of the Resurrection

We are going to come back to Luke 24 to finish the session, but take a few minutes now to think about why the resurrection is important. *Ask the group to share why they think the resurrection matters. Try to draw out the following, in no particular order:*

- It is God's confirmation that Jesus is who he said he was. The cross and resurrection were at the very heart of his plan of salvation.
- If Jesus is alive, we can know him today. Although not many people encounter the risen Christ as Paul did on the Damascus Road, many down the ages and today have seen visions of him and Christian testimony is that we know Jesus is alive because we have a personal relationship with him.
- Because of the death and resurrection of Jesus we can know forgiveness and new beginnings.
- Paul tells us in 1 Corinthians 15 and elsewhere that because Jesus is alive, we can be confident that those who are 'in Christ' and have a relationship with him

will also be raised from the dead. Death has been defeated.
- Paul also tells us that the resurrection of Jesus is the proof that evil was defeated at the cross. Although we still see evil at work in this world and experience temptation in our own lives, the resurrection assures us that Jesus has conquered all the powers of darkness and Satan is a defeated enemy.

*The testimonies on the **Video** 'The Resurrection Today' may be used at this point.*

Now go back to Luke and read 24:44-53.
Jesus could not remain forever with his disciples, appearing to them from time to time. His plans were for something far bigger than that. His plans encompassed the whole world beginning with those in Jerusalem. While he had been with them on earth, he had taught them about the gift of the Holy Spirit which he said the Father would send on them to equip them for this task. We shall be thinking more about the work of the Holy Spirit next week and some of the daily readings will help prepare us to do that. Our Chunk Reading this week is from the Acts of the Apostles and it begins with Luke retelling the story with which he ended his gospel, the story we have just read. In both, Jesus tells his disciples that he has a job for them to do but they must wait in Jerusalem until they receive the gift of the Holy Spirit. Then in a mysterious way he is taken from them and the chapter of his earthly life is ended. But not, of course, his work, the next chapter of which is about to begin.

Prayer

Spend some time praying about the themes which have emerged in this session in the way that seems best for your group. But don't forget to leave time for the administrative task which is part of this session.

Administration

Explain that the leaders would really value a Conversation with each member of the group to get to know them a bit better, find out how they are getting on with the course and answer any questions they may have but haven't wanted to ask in the group. This is not a grilling, just an opportunity for a friendly chat! It is helpful if these meetings can take place between Weeks 4 and 6 and it would be helpful to arrange them now as many people live busy lives.

Before the meeting, the leaders should have thought about which members of the group each will see and about what times they have available. Please bear in mind safeguarding principles when planning these Conversations. You need to allow about an hour and a half for each meeting though some may take less. If at all possible it is best not to try to cram too many meetings into one morning, afternoon or evening. Listening carefully to individuals and to God on their behalf can be very tiring as well as a great blessing. For more on these Conversations, please see the information which follows this chapter.

THE CONVERSATION

In choosing which leader is to see each member and deciding where they are to meet, issues regarding safeguarding have to be taken into account. The ideal is that one leader should meet with one member, but this may not always be wise or possible. Probably the best place to meet is in the comfort and privacy of the member's own home, but this may not always be appropriate and care should be taken in arranging suitable venues.

Your meeting with each member is of great importance. You will need to listen to God as well as the person you are with. It is a great privilege for you to hear people tell their own story: it may well be the first time they have ever had the opportunity to talk about these deep and very personal issues. It may not be easy for them to find the right language to express it and you may need to be patient.

The Conversation should:

1. Establish a bond of friendship between you and the group member. A relationship of trust can be established, which means that the member feels valued and heard.
2. Ensure that each individual in the group is seen as of equal worth. In group meetings it is easy to give more attention to those who talk most or who present obvious

problems. This time with each member often presents a very different picture than has been seen before in group meetings.

3. Enable each member to express their fears, feelings and expectations.

4. Help you to be aware of the spiritual position of each person before Session 6.

Tell them beforehand that while a cup of something would be welcome, they do not need to prepare anything more than that.

When you meet, do everything possible to put them at their ease. This is not an interview or an examination. Do not carry any papers—a clipboard may bring back unpleasant memories! Indicating that you are in a hurry will not help. It is just two people chatting about how they are getting on in the course and you should be prepared to describe what your own experience has been.

Assure the member of complete confidentiality between you. If they want to show you their Journal, say that you see that as a privilege, but do not ask to see it.

Try to memorise the following points and cover them in the course of your discussion—but they do not have to come up in any particular order. Ask the Holy Spirit to guide you and help you remember anything that is particularly important. They fall into three categories:

1. The Course

a) How have they found the course—stimulating/dull … informative/heard it all before … straightforward/confusing? (See Box.)

THE CONVERSATION

> *Confusion*
>
> People can find the course confusing. This is *usually* not a comment on your teaching ability but a sign of growth. When the Holy Spirit is changing our ideas, our preconceptions and even bigotry first have to be challenged before we can begin to see things with God's eyes. We often go through a period of confusion as we begin to doubt our existing position as God moves us from that position to a better one.

b) Has being together with the rest of the group been useful? Often this is one of the most positive points of the course so far.

c) How have they got on with the Journal? In what ways have they found it helpful? (It is often found that course members do the daily portions in one or two sessions during the week rather than as a daily discipline. This should not be frowned on: the important thing is that they are reading their Bible.)

2. The Impact of the Course

a) Has their experience or understanding of God changed as the course has gone on? Many people find a crystallising of their previous spiritual journey and a pattern of God's work emerges.

b) Have they got any questions arising from the course—intellectual or moral?

c) Is there anything particular on their conscience? It is important that there should be a deep understanding of repentance and a thorough self-examination before ministry. The offer of a more formal act of penitence may be appropriate.

d) Has there been any involvement with the occult? (On the one hand, avoid any inquisition which sets the person worrying about trifles, but on the other hand, explore the area sensitively. Nearly always, plain repentance and trust in Christ are the only healing required. If deliverance is indicated, *never* undertake it without consulting and working with someone else who is experienced in this field. An opportunity to discuss the occult more fully is given in Session 5.)

3. The Future

a) Are they aware of what becoming a Christian or deepening their commitment may mean in their personal lives? (There may be issues within the family or work which need articulating at this point.)

b) Are they ready to commit themselves to God and his people, remembering that none of us is ever wholly worthy?

End with a brief prayer for the person and their home situation, any people who have been mentioned, other course members and the time of ministry. If you are confident that they will know it, you could say the Lord's Prayer together. If they wish to pray aloud, so much the better.

Session 4

WHO IS THE HOLY SPIRIT?

Aim: To help people to understand the work of the Holy Spirit.

LEADING THE SESSION

Sessions 4 and 5 explore the work of the Holy Spirit in the individual and the church, both in the New Testament and today. For some church members this may be something they have never thought much about or a topic coloured by past experience—both positive and negative—and pastoral sensitivity may be required. Enquirers will usually take the material covered in these two sessions in their stride and be excited to hear about God at work today as well as in the past.

Further teaching about the gifts of the Holy Spirit is given in the next session. The gifts are one of the ways in which Jesus equips his followers to continue his mission. They played an essential part in the life of the early church and should be a normal part of church life today.

The New Testament uses the phrases 'baptism in the Spirit', 'filled with the Spirit' and 'anointed with the Spirit' fairly interchangeably, though each has a distinctive emphasis. The terminology you use in this session should be determined by what is most helpful in your local context. The Appendix explains how the authors understand the work of the Holy Spirit as part of Christian initiation. It is neither an optional extra 'for those who like that kind of thing' nor a second blessing for the elite!

The **Video** 'Session 4: The Holy Spirit Today' contains personal experiences of the Holy Spirit which may be useful in this session. Sheets containing the characteristics of being filled with the Spirit (see below) are best prepared in advance.

PRESENTATION

Begin the evening with prayer, perhaps inviting group members to offer short praises or thanksgivings, before asking the Holy Spirit to bless and guide your discussions.

Explain that you are going to begin with the Chunk Reading from last week but first ask if anyone has any questions or things they wish to share.

Recap and Introduction

Acts begins where we left off last week.

- Jesus appeared to his disciples at different times and places and continued teaching them about his mission and the task he was leaving for them to do.

- He reminded them that they would not have to continue his work in their own strength. Just as he had been filled with the Holy Spirit at his baptism and equipped for his public ministry, so they too would be filled with the Holy Spirit.
- They were to wait in Jerusalem until they had received this special gift (Acts 1:5).
- The Holy Spirit would enable them to tell people about him starting from Jerusalem and extending throughout the known world (Acts 1:8).
- After Jesus had left them, they returned to Jerusalem and met regularly for prayer with other disciples including Mary and several other women (Acts 1:14).
- They chose someone to take the place of Judas who had betrayed Jesus. Twelve was a very significant number for the Jews because there were twelve tribes of Israel, and it was no accident that Jesus had originally chosen twelve disciples to be particularly close to him and travel with him. Choosing Matthias by lot would not have seemed as strange to them as it does to us. We know very little about what happened to any of the Twelve except Peter and John. From chapter 13, Acts focuses on Paul and his companions as they take the good news of Jesus to the Gentile world.

The Day of Pentecost

Invite the group to open their Bibles at Acts 2. Although most will have read this as part of the Chunk Reading, it would be good to refresh their memories by reading 2:1-16 again now. (Ask someone you know will read well as this is an important and dramatic passage.) Explain that Pentecost was one of the major Jewish harvest festivals and there would have been large crowds of pilgrims in Jerusalem from all around the Mediterranean.

What strikes you from these verses? What questions do you have? *Perhaps invite them to talk to their neighbour before discussing in the whole group.*

The order in which these points emerge is not important, but before moving on, the following should be explored:

- Something dramatic happened which they could only describe as being 'like' wind and fire. (Often we can only use picture language when trying to describe spiritual experience.)
- Each one of them was filled with the Holy Spirit, not just the Twelve.
- They began to speak in other languages. This is sometimes known as the gift of tongues. At Pentecost it was a gift that enabled them to both praise God and communicate with the crowds.

WHO IS THE HOLY SPIRIT?

- A crowd gathered to find out what was going on. They were amazed and confused. They had never seen anything like it before. There was such an uproar that some people thought the disciples must be drunk!
- The believers were speaking about the wonderful things God had done.
- Peter, who only a few weeks before had been afraid to admit to a slave girl that he even knew Jesus, came forward and addressed the potentially hostile crowd with confidence and authority.

It is probably best not to read the whole of Peter's speech at this point. Instead point out:

- He says that what has happened was predicted in the Old Testament by the prophet Joel. God has poured out his Spirit on everyone, not just special people (2:17-18, 21).
- He talks about Jesus and how God had worked through him (2:22).
- How it was part of God's plan that Jesus should be crucified and raised back to life and that both the Jews and the Gentiles were responsible for his death (2:23-24).
- That Jesus was the Messiah the Jews had been waiting for (2:25-31).
- That having been raised from the dead (which they could witness to because they had met with him), Jesus was now exalted to the place of honour at God's

right hand (2:32-36) and it was from there that he had poured out his Holy Spirit.

Now read 2:37-41. **What effect did Peter's sermon have on the crowds?**

- They were deeply moved and wanted to know how to respond.
- Peter said each person must take responsibility for themselves, repent, turn to God and be baptised for the forgiveness of their sins.
- Then they too would receive the Holy Spirit.
- He went on speaking and pressing home his point.
- About three thousand people responded and were baptised!

Now read Acts 2:42-47. **What strikes you about this first Christian community?**

- They were very committed to learning more, sharing with one another in fellowship, food and the Lord's Supper (i.e., what we often call Holy Communion), and praying together (2:42).
- The miraculous was normal, as it had been in the ministry of Jesus.
- They shared their possessions (2:45).
- They worshipped together in the Temple and in homes (2:46).

WHO IS THE HOLY SPIRIT?

- Their characteristic was joy (2:46-47).
- They were well thought of and grew day by day as God added to their number (2:47).

The Spirit Today

The Holy Spirit was not just given to the first disciples. Jesus promised to give the Holy Spirit to all who believe in him. He still gives the Holy Spirit to people who believe in him today.

Here, if possible, the group leaders should share briefly their experience of the work of the Holy Spirit. Alternatively, the testimonies on the **Video** *'The Holy Spirit Today' could be used at this point.*

The important things to stress are:
- The difference the Holy Spirit makes to our lives and our faith.
- This is God's gift and is given as God chooses but is freely available for all.
- There is no one blueprint which is followed by everyone. Some people have a dramatic and life-changing experience of being filled with the Holy Spirit, but for many others the experience is very quiet and the changes more gradual.
- It is the surrender to God that lies at the heart of being filled with the Spirit which is most important.

It may be that other members of the group have had experiences of the Spirit's work which they can share.

As we look at the New Testament and the experience of Christians through the ages, we discover certain common characteristics of being filled with the Spirit. *Sheets of A4 containing the words in bold should have been prepared in advance unless one of the leaders has very clear handwriting and can write as you go along.*

- When we ask God to fill us with his Holy Spirit, **something definite takes place**. For the first disciples it meant an overwhelming experience which could only be described as 'wind' and 'fire'. For some other people (as in the testimonies?) it may be far less dramatic. Nevertheless, God longs to give us this gift and always responds when we ask him. No two people's experience will ever be exactly the same. God deals with each of us differently as he knows what is best for each one of us. Nonetheless, one cannot be filled with the Holy Spirit imperceptibly.
- When we are filled with the Spirit, **we will change**.
- It may be that like Peter on the day of Pentecost, we find we have a **new confidence to speak about Jesus**. All of us will grow in our faith and assurance of God's love.
- For all of us the Holy Spirit begins to make us more like Jesus. Paul calls this **the fruit of the Holy Spirit** and we shall think a bit more about this next week.
- We will be equipped to serve God and other people through the different **gifts of the Holy Spirit**. Again, more about this next week.
- Just like the first believers on the day of Pentecost, we will find ourselves **drawn towards other Christians** in

worship, sharing and prayer. This togetherness is called 'fellowship'.

- Just like those first Christians, we will find **a growing hunger to learn** more about God through studying the Scriptures and through prayer.

A Note about Tongues

Speaking in tongues, one of the gifts of the Spirit mentioned at Pentecost, may be intriguing for some and for others threatening. Do not over-emphasise this, but if there are questions share your experiences if you have any and reassure them:

- Praying in tongues is as much under our control as if we were praying in English.
- We don't have to be in an emotionally or spiritually exalted state to speak in tongues.
- It is a prayer language and is used in several ways: to praise God; to intercede for others; with the gift of interpretation to convey God's message in a particular situation; occasionally to speak directly to people in their own language. Although sometimes used publicly, it is most often used in private prayer.
- We don't understand it, but it does us good!

There will be an opportunity to talk further about tongues next week when we look at the gifts of the Spirit.

Prayer

Finish with a relaxed time of prayer thanking God for the gift of the Holy Spirit. Be open to the Spirit giving words of prophecy or pictures or tongues and interpretation.

Administration

Explain the Journal exercises for this week and check that the arrangements made last week for the Conversations are still all right. Encourage group members to jot down any questions they want to ask or any personal matter which they may want to talk about but reassure them that this is not an inspection, just a friendly chat so you can get to know one another a bit better and make sure they can get the most from the course. While a cup of tea or coffee would be welcome, please don't go to any trouble.

Session 5

HARVEST TIME: FRUIT AND GIFTS

Aims:

- To teach about the fruit and gifts of the Holy Spirit.
- To help group members prepare for Session 6 where they will have the opportunity to respond to what they have discovered on the course so far.

LEADING THE SESSION

There is a lot to cover in this session so keep an eye on the timing so as not to cut short the important teaching about repentance and faith.

There is a danger that the fruit of the Spirit may be seen as less interesting than the gifts, particularly as the latter may be new to some group members. Developing the fruit of the Spirit is important if the gifts are to be used well and appropriately, so this section should not be skimped.

The **Video** 'Session 5, A. The Gifts of the Spirit' gives teaching on the gifts of the Spirit in a concise way. Using this may free up more time for discussion. There are also testimonies about how the gifts function in the lives of individuals and the church which may be used to supplement the experience of group leaders if necessary ('Session 5, B. Experiencing the Gifts'). You could invite one or two church members to give their testimony, but be aware that there is a lot to cover in this session and inviting others to join you will inevitably draw things out further.

The group should be beginning to look forward to Session 6 even if some are apprehensive. Encourage a calm expectancy and openness to what God has to give. It would be helpful to read through the 'Practicalities' in the next session and decide on things like where you will meet so that you can tell the group at the end of this session.

You will need to prepare different illustrations for this session:
- A4 sheets with a part of the fruit of the Spirit on each one;
- the papers with the characteristics of Jesus from Session 2;
- either a set of tools or pictures of tools for teaching about the gifts of the Spirit;
- pens and paper to illustrate repentance.

PRESENTATION

Introduction

Ask if anyone has any comments or questions arising from the Journal work. It may be good at this stage to ask what group members are finding helpful and why.

HARVEST TIME: FRUIT AND GIFTS

Prayer

Pray that we may all grow in our understanding of the work of the Holy Spirit in our lives.

The Fruit of the Spirit

Last week we began to think about the changes brought about in our lives by the Holy Spirit. Has anything happened this week which is encouraging and an indication that the Spirit is already at work in your life, bringing about change?

Allow a brief time for sharing. It may be helpful to ask the group to think back to the beginning of the course and think about any changes or good things that have happened since then. Often the group will be very encouraged when they discover what is already happening in their lives or, more often, what they see happening in the lives of other group members. Such a time of sharing can lead naturally into a time of thanksgiving with individuals contributing short prayers.

Read Galatians 5:19-26. As you do so, one of the leaders should put the A4 sheets with the fruit on the floor in the middle of the group.

Paul contrasts what happens when people follow 'the desires of [our] sinful nature' with the fruit that the Holy Spirit produces in our lives. God wants us to become more and more like his Son, Jesus (Romans 8:29). The fruit of the Spirit is the character of Jesus being produced in his people. This doesn't make us clones of Jesus but rather allows his character to be formed within the unique personality God has given each one of us. *Take a moment to look at the fruit of the Spirit and ask if anyone has any questions or comments.*

Now produce the bits of paper from Session 2 and put them alongside the fruit of the Spirit. Discuss how they dovetail.

Think for a minute about fruit.
- Fruit is the natural product of a healthy tree. Effort is not required on the part of the tree to produce fruit! Our characters will become more like Jesus by our remaining in him, not by strenuous self-improvement techniques like dieting (John 15:4-5). Part of remaining in him is about being honest with him about our failings and the way we want to change. But the power to change comes from the Holy Spirit working in us. This is particularly important for anyone who has undertaken any self-improvement programme and failed. Change comes as a result of God's grace working in us at our request.
- Fruit is more often seen by the onlooker: others are often far more aware of the changes in us than we are in ourselves. Perhaps some members have already had comments from friends or family about how they are changing since coming on this course or being linked with the church.

The Gifts of the Spirit

Last session we noted the important place of signs and wonders in the life of the early church and may have spent some time talking about the gift of tongues. *Ask the group what signs and wonders they have noted as they have done their Chunk Reading of Acts. As well as the general references (2:43; 5:15; 6:8; 8:6-7; 8:13) they may mention the lame man at the Temple (3:1-10), Ananias and Sapphira (5:1-11), the conversion of Saul (9:1-19), Aeneas (9:33-34), Tabitha/Dorcas (9:37-41), Cornelius (10:3-6), Peter (10:11-16) and those listening to his address (10:44-47), the prophets from Jerusalem (11:27-30), Peter's release from prison (12:6-11) or the death of Herod (12:20-23). Don't look at all these references; they are listed here simply as a reminder for you.*

Many of these stories are dramatic, but the gifts of the Spirit are not necessarily dramatic. They are simply the tool kit God has given us as we go about his business in the world.

The following teaching about the toolbox and the gifts of the Spirit in 1 Corinthians 12 is given succinctly on the **Video** *'Session 5, A. The Gifts of the Spirit' and you are encouraged to use it and then discuss what the group has heard.*

Bring out the visual aid prepared before the session and read 1 Corinthians 12:4-11.

In this passage we have a list of nine of the gifts of the Spirit. This is not comprehensive. There are other lists of gifts mentioned in Romans 12 and Ephesians 4 as well as other individual gifts mentioned throughout the New Testament. Note that in each of the places where Paul lists gifts of the Spirit it is in the context of teaching about the church as the body of Christ. The gifts are given to individuals for building up the church and ministering in the world.

From 1 Corinthians 12:4-7 note:

- There are different kinds of gifts and of service and different ways in which God uses individuals—different people need different tools for different jobs.

- They all come from the same source, God working through his Holy Spirit.
- The gifts are given so that we can help one another. **They are not trophies or toys but tools** which are meant to be used to do something constructive for the benefit of others.

Look briefly at each gift in turn and, where possible, give examples from your own experience, but be careful to do so in a way that other people can't be identified. (Remember, not everyone has every gift, but you may have seen someone else exercising a particular gift effectively.)

There will probably be some in the group who have had the experience of being in the right place at the right time and saying just the right thing which has really helped someone else. They may be unaware that they have been exercising gifts of wisdom and knowledge. (This is surprisingly common and helps the group to understand that the gifts are useful rather than spooky.) Ask the group if they have experience using any of the gifts or any of the gifts being used.

It is important when talking about the gifts of the Spirit that our examples should be as down-to-earth as possible. Although there may be times when we experience a dramatic healing or powerful prophecy, most of the time the gifts are the tool kit of the jobbing Christian getting on with their daily lives.

As well as teaching about the gifts from 1 Corinthians 12, the **Video** *'Session 5, B. Experiencing the Gifts' contains some testimonies of different gifts being used.*

HARVEST TIME: FRUIT AND GIFTS

Preparing to Receive

It is important to leave enough time for this section as it seeks to help prepare people for the ministry time in the next session.

God does not want us simply to talk about new life in Jesus and the fruit and gifts of the Spirit. He wants us to know these things for ourselves. In Acts 2:37, which we looked at last session, the crowd asked Peter and the others, 'What should we do?' Peter replied, 'Each of you must repent of your sins and turn to God, and be baptized in the name of Jesus Christ for the forgiveness of your sins. Then you will receive the gift of the Holy Spirit. This promise is to you, to your children, and to those far away' (vv. 38-39). In other words, this is for everyone.

Peter was talking about repentance and faith or trust in God. We shall look briefly at each in turn.

Repentance

Repentance is a change of direction:

- A conscious turning away from things which spoil our relationship with God.
- A turning towards God.

The following teaching can be easily illustrated by a visual aid drawn at the time. First draw a circle representing our life with a capital 'I' at the centre. This represents the self at the centre which spoils our relationship with God. The second action can be demonstrated by putting a line through the 'I' thus turning it into a cross representing

Jesus at the centre of our lives. This links in with the four circles of Session 2.

What we are turning away from is our self-centredness which puts 'I' at the centre of our lives. This is what the Bible calls sin. But the Bible also talks about specific sins. We have read a list of specific sins already in Galatians 5:19-21. Notice the scope of this list: it includes everything from sorcery and sexual immorality to jealousy and outbursts of anger. These are not the only sins; other lists in the New Testament are different but similarly wide ranging. As Jesus said when he talked about taking the speck out of another's eye while not noticing the plank in our own, it is often easier to acknowledge the faults of others than admit our own. Repentance is a decision we make, not simply a response to a feeling of guilt.

It is important if we want to make a new start with God, whether for the first time or for the thousandth time, to examine ourselves and ask the Holy Spirit to show us whether there is anything in particular which is spoiling our relationship with God.

There are certain things such as occult practices which some may have engaged in 'innocently' given their prevalence in our society, which are specifically forbidden in Scripture and can impose lasting spiritual damage if not specifically confessed and renounced. Others may be aware of certain practices which seem to have such an unshakable grip on their lives that they have become addictions. If members are aware of things which fall into either of these categories or other things from the past which weigh heavily upon them, encourage them to mention them in the Conversations if these are yet to happen or to have a brief word with one of the leaders.

Faith or Trust

We exercise faith every day of our lives: when we sit on a chair and expect it to hold us, follow our sat nav and expect it to get us to our destination, believe the 'expert' we hear on the television or trust a friend or relative to do what they have promised. Some things in which we put our faith or trust are more reliable than others!

On the day of Pentecost, Peter invited people to be baptised as a sign of putting their trust in Jesus Christ as Lord and Saviour. In other words, accepting all that Jesus had done for them through his death and resurrection. Faith is trusting in God and relying on him and accepting that his promises of love, forgiveness and new life are true for us personally. Faith, like repentance, is a decision we take to trust in God rather than in ourselves or anything else. It is a decision to put God at the centre of our lives.

If you think that you may want to use these or similar baptism promises as part of the ministry time in Session 6, then it may be worth mentioning them now:

> **I repent of my sins … I renounce evil … I turn to Christ**

This is not the point at which to get into a detailed discussion of baptism. Depending on their backgrounds there may be some within the group who were baptised as infants but who have never acknowledged the promises made on their behalf for themselves. The time of ministry next session is an ideal opportunity for them to do so. Equally, there may be some on the course who have never been baptised. There are plenty of examples in the New Testament of baptism in water being separated from the decision to believe in Jesus and trust him. Those who have completed Saints Alive! often choose to be baptised or renew their baptism promises when the course has ended.

> Peter said that if people repented and believed then:
> - **Their sins would be forgiven.**
> - **They would receive God's gift, the Holy Spirit.**

The people believed what he had said and repented and trusted in God. Our Christian lives do not depend on our feelings at any particular time but on the character and promises of God. Of the three thousand who were baptised at Pentecost, some would have felt deeply moved, some would have been convinced by Peter's words and some would have just felt this was the right thing to do. For all of them, it was a decision that changed their lives.

Next Week

At next week's session there will be an opportunity to respond to what we have heard over the last few weeks. *(The pattern of the session will not be the same as usual so it will be helpful for course members to know what is going to happen.)*

After a short time of teaching, everyone who wishes can dedicate their lives to God through Jesus Christ and receive the laying on of hands with prayer to be filled with the Holy Spirit. Those who are already Christians and who know the fulness of the Spirit will also have the opportunity to rededicate their lives, be filled afresh with the Holy Spirit and pray for their ministry within the body of Christ.

Explain in broad outline the mechanics of the next session: where people are to meet if different from normal; that there will be the opportunity to receive prayer and the laying on of hands; that there is no compulsion for anyone to receive ministry and that if someone doesn't feel ready to take that step at this point they should still come along and support those in the group who do. People may decide to leave at different times and it is likely that some may be later home than normal depending on the size of your group. Because it is difficult to know how long the session will last, any who are normally picked up by a husband/wife may be better making arrangements for a lift with another group member.

Journal and Administration

Check that everyone who has not yet had their Conversation knows when and where it will take place and encourage everyone to use their Journal as they prepare for next week.

Prayer

Praise God for his love and pray specifically that at the next session everyone will take the step towards God that he wants of them. Aim to build up faith and expectancy. Be open to exercising the gifts of the Spirit.

Session 6

TIME FOR MINISTRY

Aims:

- To offer brief teaching on receiving the Holy Spirit.
- To offer an opportunity for each member to respond and receive appropriate ministry.

LEADING THE SESSION

This session is different from every other. In many ways it is the key session of the course and you will need to pray for great sensitivity in leading it. Prior to the session you should be praying earnestly for each person that they would take the step or steps towards God which are right for them at this time. Your Conversations with course members should help you discern what to pray.

Before the course you prayed that the right people would come on it. No one is here by mistake! God longs to bless them, so it is essential that you offer each one the opportunity for response. To omit to offer ministry at this point is to sell them short and amounts to pastoral failure no matter how anxious you are. In practice it has been found that the vast majority of people come forward for prayer during this session.

It is natural for leaders to feel more anxious than usual about this session. In many ways we are stepping back and allowing God to work directly in people's lives. We have to be flexible in our leadership and responsive to the Holy Spirit.

If you have a large group, you may want to ask others to help you pray for people. Ideally this should be other Christians from within the group. If you have to invite others who have not been part of the group, it would be good if they could at least come and take part in Session 5 as well. They should be paired with one of the group leaders. However, introducing others at this point can alter the dynamics and trust between you and group members which have built up throughout the course.

Prayer

If possible, those involved in ministry should meet together before this session in the place where ministry will be offered. It is good for the leaders to pray for one another before the session starts, but it is important for you to be seen to pray for one another immediately before you invite others to ask for ministry. This models the truth that we all need more of God and demonstrates that ministry itself is not too scary and anyone can do it.

Practicalities

While there is a sense in which some aspects of ministry can never be planned, thinking through the practical arrangements for this session is essential. Here are some factors to consider:

- **Reasonable privacy**—so that the individual can talk quietly without being overheard.
- **Accessibility**—it is hard to lay hands on someone in the middle of a sofa!
- **Freedom to respond**—individuals should not feel undue pressure to respond. Some encouragement for individuals we know want to come forward may be necessary.
- **Surroundings**—elements of peace and beauty are helpful as the place where they receive ministry will become 'holy ground' for some course members.

It is possible for ministry to take place in the usual meeting room. However, addressing these practical considerations is usually difficult, especially if sessions happen in a home. In practice the best locations have been found to be a church or larger meeting room set out especially for the purpose with facilities for quiet music to play in the background and refreshments to be available. (For some people there can be quite a lot of waiting around in this session and the opportunity to make themselves a cup of tea or coffee can be helpful.) A church is ideal because people can meet together for the initial teaching, be invited to spread themselves out if they want to while waiting for ministry and come forward to the altar rail or specially

TIME FOR MINISTRY

set-up prayer point when ready. The same facilities can be created within a hall or meeting room. Depending on where you are meeting, you will need to think through whether you are sitting alongside the person or, if using the altar rail, whether you are going to kneel opposite them or alongside them when you pray for them.

Remember that people will be sitting still for some time so good heating is essential.

Timing

The timing of this session is both difficult and important. The teaching at the beginning should be kept brief. Most members will have read the passages in their Journals before coming.

Remember that you are offering prayer ministry, not counselling. There should not be the need for lots of talking with individuals. That has happened in the Conversation. However, time can fly by when we are praying for people and leaders need to be aware of those waiting around to come for prayer or anxiety levels will begin to rise.

Who Prays?

Ideally the leaders, joined by assistant leaders if you have them, should pray in pairs. One can lead in praying while the other listens to the Lord for specific words of wisdom, pictures or prophecy. If others have been asked to assist, they should each work with one of the leaders. If others within the group have been asked to assist with ministry, they should come forward for prayer first and this should be explained to the rest of the group. If time demands and leaders are confident enough, it may be necessary for the leaders to separate and pray individually in which case it can be helpful to invite someone who has already received prayer to help them.

PRESENTATION

Begin with a brief prayer but don't ask about questions arising from Journals as most will have had Conversations recently.

Luke 11:1-13
This passage and the next one give 'instructions' on receiving the Holy Spirit. *These elements should be highlighted and can then be referred to during the time of ministry.*

After reading the passage, make the following points:
- The disciples had a desire for a deeper experience of God (11:1).
- There is a need for persistence and seriousness of purpose in asking for the Spirit as in all prayer (11:5-8). This parable is not about God's reluctance to give!
- The promise is sure—those who ask will receive (11:9-10). The Spirit is received by faith, not feelings.
- God never gives us dangerous or inappropriate gifts (11:11-12). Therefore we should not fear any gift from our heavenly Father. (The parallel passage in Matthew 7:11 talks about 'good gifts'.)
- We must ask for the Spirit to be given to us (11:13). Being filled with the Spirit rarely happens spontaneously.

TIME FOR MINISTRY

John 7:37-39

- 7:37 speaks of three stages: thirsting, coming and drinking. This can be illustrated with a glass of water. It is no good asking for it if we don't then take it and drink from it!
- 7:38 shows that streams go out from the Spirit-filled person into the world. We are not given the Spirit solely for ourselves. We are to be a spiritual oasis in the desert.

Instructions

Explain to group members what is going to happen next:

- *where you want them to sit;*
- *what you want them to do (pray for themselves and other members of the group);*
- *when and where they should come forward for ministry;*
- *explain that the leaders will pray for one another first (if that is what you are doing);*
- *encourage them not to wait too long before coming forward as everyone needs to have the opportunity to receive prayer!*
- *invite them to help themselves to refreshments at any time;*
- *explain that though some may want to stay to the end, people are free to leave at any time;*
- *you will pray differently with each person, but everyone will be asked if they want to offer their lives to God either for the first time or in rededication, and each person will*

be offered the laying on of hands with prayer for the filling of the Spirit.

Check before you split that people have understood the instructions.

The Time of Ministry

While it is impossible to set out a blueprint of how to minister to each person, the following outline has been found to be helpful. It is based round the three promises of baptism mentioned in Session 5. Many find the semi-formal structure helpful as it enables those receiving prayer to start to speak. However, this may not be appropriate in your context and something more informal may seem more natural. The important thing is to enable each person to offer themselves afresh to God in dedication.

- Ask the person if they wish to repent of the past and begin afresh. If so they may find it helpful to say aloud after you, **'I repent of my sins'.**
- Ask them if they need to get rid of any wrong things from the past which still have an influence of power over them. **'I renounce evil.'**
- Then ask them if they want to dedicate their life to Christ. **'I turn to Christ.'**
- Invite them, if they want to, to put that prayer of dedication into their own words.
- Then ask if they wish to be **filled with the Holy Spirit**. If they say 'yes' then lay hands gently but firmly on their head (you may need to stand to do this) and ask God to fill

them completely with the gift of the Holy Spirit. Take your time over this and be guided by the Holy Spirit. It can be helpful to encourage someone to praise God out loud as this takes their focus away from themselves and puts it on God. Sometimes at this point people may begin to pray in tongues and should be encouraged to speak out if this is the case. Do not be alarmed if there are physical manifestations as the Holy Spirit releases pent-up emotions—crying, laughing, shaking or resting in the Spirit are all quite common.

- *Whether or not there are obvious signs of God's action, thank God for filling them with the Holy Spirit and pray that they may be given every spiritual gift they need to serve him and bless others.*
- *It may be that you are aware from the Conversation that there is something in particular for which the person would appreciate prayer. Otherwise it can be helpful to ask the person if there is anything else for which they would like to receive prayer.*
- *Before concluding, listen to God for any prophetic words or pictures or verses of Scripture which would encourage the person who has been prayed for.*
- *Encourage them to spend some time in quiet prayer before leaving when they feel ready.*

Conclusion

Often some of the group will have left before you have prayed for everyone. Others may be sharing or praying with one another. Once everyone has received prayer, draw together those who are left for a brief prayer of thanksgiving and blessing.

Tidy up and go home because you will be tired, but meet as soon as you can to pray for members of the group and be alert to opportunities just to touch base with them before the next session.

Be Prepared

There are various things which leaders need to consider in planning the last part of the course. Please read through Sessions 7-9 and decide in particular how you might use 'The Church Member' material in Session 8 and which of the options for Session 9 you feel would work best for your group. If any form of 'Party with a Purpose' is planned, course members will need information about this at the end of Session 7.

On the Video you will find a selection of brief testimonies about growing in faith and belonging to the church. You will find it helpful to familiarise yourself with these so that you can draw on them as appropriate.

Session 7

GROWING UP

Aims:

- To help people reflect on what they experienced during Session 6.
- To encourage them to base their faith on the facts of the gospel, not feelings.
- To begin to lay foundations for continuing growth in Christ.

LEADING THE SESSION

Often people will begin sharing as they gather together. Don't interrupt this in order to have a formal beginning and prayer. Encourage everyone to participate and listen carefully to the stories that are being told so that you can link them in with the teaching later in the session.

Just as Peter explained what had been happening to the crowd at Pentecost, so we need to help people interpret their experience.

This session needs sensitivity because of the variety of experiences members may have had. Some may feel magnificent, still overwhelmed by what they experienced during ministry. Others may have come down-to-earth with a bump and doubt the reality of their experience. Others may have had a feeling of anti-climax because it wasn't as they expected while others may be quietly rejoicing knowing that they have a new or deeper relationship with God. It is important that the enthusiasm of the joyful is not allowed to swamp the confusion of the disappointed. Some may not have received ministry at all. If appropriate, they can be offered prayer at the end of this session or on another occasion when the time is right.

The session will work best if the teaching is given in response to the experiences within the group, which may mean the subjects arise in a different order from that outlined here. However, keep an eye on the time because everything in this session is important, however succinctly you have to cover it.

In looking at Worship in the means of growth section, you can take the opportunity to explain briefly your church's practice on baptism, confirmation, membership, Communion, etc., but it is unwise to get too immersed in the subject. It may be right here to talk about your church's usual pattern of initiation if it is likely to apply personally to any in your group.

The bookmarks, 'coin' and the wheel of growth will need to be prepared in advance.

Be aware of the testimonies on the **Video** 'Session 7: Growing Up' in case you wish to draw on any of them.

PRESENTATION

Sharing and Discussion

Invite group members to share what God has been doing in their lives over the past week including the difficulties and disappointments they may have had. Although joy will be the predominant note of this session, watch out for any who are not sharing it and be prepared to pray with them afterwards if appropriate.

If people can articulate the work of Christ in their lives within the group, it will be easier for them to speak of him outside.

Do not rush this part of the session but watch for opportunities to bring in some of the teaching covered later.

Facts and Feelings

Read 1 John 5:13.

God wants us to be confident that we are Christians. John's first letter was written to assure us of that.

Feelings may come and go but our faith is founded on fact:
- The fact of Christ's incarnation, death and resurrection.
- The promises of God found in Scripture.
- The fact of our profession of faith (made either in the ministry time last week or on another occasion).
- The public profession of faith at baptism/confirmation/being received into fellowship reinforces this and makes it more objective.

Jesus promises not only to welcome and receive us if we come to him, he also promises to stay with us and reassures us that we have new life in him:

- 'Those the Father has given me will come to me, and I will never reject them' (John 6:37).
- 'I am with you always' (Matthew 28:20).
- 'Look! I stand at the door and knock. If you hear my voice and open the door, I will come in, and we will share a meal together as friends' (Revelation 3:20).
- 'Anyone who belongs to Christ has become a new person. The old life is gone; a new life has begun!' (2 Corinthians 5:17).
- 'God has said, "I will never fail you. I will never abandon you." So we can say with confidence, "The LORD is my helper, so I will have no fear. What can mere people do to me?"' (Hebrews 13:5b-6).

Have some cards or bookmarks prepared with Hebrews 13:5b-6 written on them ready for each member together with the name and date of the course. The other verses are all in the Journal (page 110), and it can be suggested that course members learn them by heart.

End this section with prayer giving thanks for God's faithfulness and for what each person has received so far during the course. Pray that they may grow in confidence in their identity in Christ. (It might be good to invite members of the group to pray, giving thanks at this point, but the leaders should pray for assurance and growth in faith.)

Afterwards—Difficulties and Opportunities

What happens once we have become a Christian or been freshly filled with the Holy Spirit?

Remind the group that, after his baptism, 'Jesus, full of the Holy Spirit, ... was led by the Spirit in the wilderness, where he was tempted by the devil for forty days' (Luke 4:1-2).

Whenever we take a significant move forward in our relationship with God, there will be both difficulties and opportunities. *Produce a simple visual aid made earlier—a large coin-shaped piece of paper with 'Difficulties' on one side and 'Opportunities' on the other and space to write in examples. Don't take too long over this and, if possible, use examples shared earlier in the meeting.*

Difficulties may include:

- **Being misunderstood**—by family or friends. *There can sometimes be tensions between couples when one has been on the course and the other hasn't.*
- **Having doubts and fears**—we all do from time to time. Remember the disciples after the resurrection.
- **Feeling guilty**—as our consciences become more sensitive to sin or the Holy Spirit brings to the surface things from the past which need dealing with. *Remind them that God is always ready to forgive (1 John 1:9) and that there is no condemnation for those who belong to Christ Jesus (Romans 8:1).*
- **Experiencing challenges**—life doesn't always run smoothly and becoming a Christian does not ensure us

of an easy passage—on the contrary! But we are given a new strength to deal with difficulties and they can be used constructively (James 1:2-5).

If we ask God to use us then **Opportunities** may include:

- **Sharing our faith**—as people ask questions or notice how we are changing.
- **Helping others**—demonstrating God's love in practical ways.
- **Praying for others**—and seeing God answer prayer.
- **Seeing God work through us**—as we begin to grow in the gifts of the Spirit.

Growing as a Christian

Read John 15:1-10 and ask the group what strikes them as important from this passage. We are intended to grow and be fruitful, but if this is to happen we need to stay close to Jesus.

Healthy plants need a variety of nutrients, the right conditions for growth and a gardener looking after them. Father God is the gardener, but he also uses other members of the church, especially leaders, to help us to grow.

Produce the 'wheel of growth'. God has provided means by which we can receive his goodness and grow closer to him. If it is to run smoothly, then all the spokes are of equal importance. *Look briefly at each one, but depending on how much time has been taken with sharing, you may not be able to cover them in depth. Be ready to give examples*

GROWING UP 117

from your context of how group members may engage with and grow in these six aspects of the life of faith. There are examples on the **Video** *'Session 7—Growing Up'.*

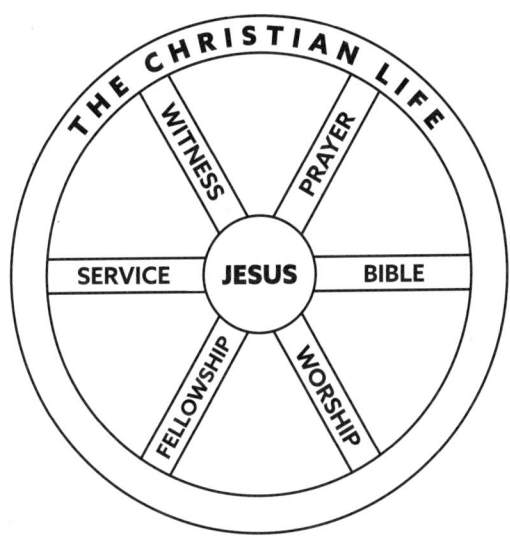

- **Prayer**—both personal daily prayer in the way we have encouraged through the Journal and by joining with others for prayer. We need to develop ways of praying and patterns of prayer that are right for us. Pray as you can, not as you can't.
- **Bible**—both reading the Bible regularly for ourselves, possibly with the aid of Bible reading notes or apps, and joining in Bible study with others. *There is information at the end of this session in the Journal about various internet sites and apps that people may find helpful, but leaders should be prepared to share resources they use and want to recommend.*

- **Worship**—meeting regularly with other Christians for worship, prayer and teaching. Jesus commanded us to share bread and wine as he did with his first disciples. The Lord's Supper or Holy Communion is one very important way of meeting with Jesus and being fed and strengthened by him.
- **Fellowship**—meeting with other Christians to encourage one another in the faith. This is different from simply having a coffee and chat after a service. *This might be a good point at which to mention briefly any house groups or other fellowship groups which meet regularly.*
- **Service**—we have been filled with the Holy Spirit so that we can work with Jesus for the coming of his kingdom. We have been equipped with the gifts of the Spirit as tools. Some service is best done alongside other people.
- **Witness**—praying for courage and taking the opportunities God gives us to share our faith.

There is more about some of these six spokes in the Journal, and we shall have an opportunity to talk further about some of them next week when we begin to think about what it means to be church.

Administration

If you have decided to hold a 'Party with a Purpose' in Session 9, group members will need details so they can invite family and friends. If a Meal and Communion has been decided upon, then it is worth telling people at this point so they can begin thinking before the next session about what food they might like to bring.

Prayer

Try to leave enough time for some extended prayer and listening to God together. Encourage people to listen to God for words of encouragement or prophetic pictures or scriptures and then leave sufficient silence for them to do so. Remember to offer ministry to anyone who missed out last week (or arrange another time to do so) and pray about anything specific which has been shared during this session.

Session 8

BEING CHURCH

Aims:

- To teach about the importance of being part of the church.
- To encourage course members to begin to explore their ministries.
- To introduce what will happen once the course ends.

LEADING THE SESSION

This session marks a change of gear. So far we have focused mostly on the individual and their relationship with God. Now we begin to think more corporately and outwardly as we think about being part of the church and our witness and service in the world. In some groups the majority of members will already think of themselves as part of the church whereas for others this may be relatively new territory. If you are working within the context of a fresh expression type of church, you may need to adapt some of what follows for your particular context. An editable version of the commitment can be found on the website https://saintsalivecourse.com.

In order to encourage a sense of personal responsibility for others, this session includes an opportunity for commitment to the local church. It has been found that members take this with all seriousness and the opportunity should not be missed. We should not sell the church short or be apologetic about it. The benefits of Christian fellowship are so important that we are depriving people of something of great value if we hold back on this even if you need to alter the wording of the document to suit local circumstances.

Well before this session, you should give some thought to the possible ways of marking this commitment. If you are not church leaders, or there are some leaders who are not part of this course, it would be good to talk this through with them as part of the exploration.

- It can be made within the group and marked by prayer for every member who wishes to make a commitment.
- It can be marked in some way within the whole church. For instance, some churches have produced the commitment (later in this session) on good quality paper and rolled it like a scroll. These can be signed by group members and presented within a service. This can offer an opportunity to talk about the course, and perhaps some group members can give brief testimonies. The whole church can then give thanks and pray for the members as the course draws to a close.

- If some members of the group are making a public act of commitment—e.g., in a baptism, membership or confirmation service—perhaps everyone who has been on the course could be offered the opportunity to rededicate themselves by presenting them within the service.

By this time in the course, members will know each other well and be much more free in voicing their opinions. Encourage this and help people to listen and respond to each other rather than having everything addressed to the leaders. As Romans 12 reminds us, each person has something to contribute.

Often by this stage in the course, members are becoming anxious about what will happen next. They have enjoyed the teaching and the fellowship and the opportunity to pray together. Hopefully you will already have thought through the options, preferably before the course began. (See pages 29-30 for suggestions.) Now is the time to talk more specifically with the group about them so that the inevitable disappointment that the course is ending can give way to excitement about what is to follow.

Hopefully you will also have begun thinking about next week and the two options for ending the course:

- To concentrate on fellowship and thanksgiving with a shared meal and simple Communion service.
- To emphasise witness by throwing a 'Party with a Purpose'. Course members are encouraged to invite relatives and friends to a party where they can share what being on Saints Alive! has meant to them with a

view to recruiting members to a new group to start in a few weeks' time.
- It is possible to do both if a party at a later stage is used to invite people who are interested in joining a course to discover more (see Introduction and pages 39-44).
- Other approaches to Session 9 are included in the introduction to that session.

Be aware of the testimonies on the **Video** from last week in case you wish to draw on any of them in this session. Where you do so is up to you. There is also a brief testimony about the impact of a loving church on the **Video** at 'Session 8—Being Church'.

You might like to take a group photo either at the end of this session or next week.

PRESENTATION

Welcome and Introduction

Give plenty of opportunity for group members to share if they have experienced any of the things you discussed last week. Pray about these as well as for this session, encouraging as much participation from members of the group as possible.

The Body of Christ

Ask the members what it has meant to be part of this group. Spend some time discussing this, e.g.,

- *Have they learned things in the group they might not have learned on their own?*
- *Have they benefitted from the support of other group members?*
- *What have they learned about ways in which fellowship can be helped or hindered? How can such fellowship be maintained?*

When we become Christians we become part of a body—one of the terms used in the New Testament to describe the church. It was the picture used by Paul in 1 Corinthians 12 when we were thinking about the gifts of the Spirit. In this session we are going to look at a similar passage in Romans.

Read Romans 12:4-5 and ask what strikes members of the group. Make sure that in the discussion you cover the following points:

- *There are many different parts to a body but they all belong (v. 4).*
- *Each part has its own job to do. You can illustrate this using your own arms, eyes, etc.*
- *There is an essential unity in Christ (v. 5) which all Christians share. We may not always like our fellow Christians and would not necessarily choose them as friends, but they are family and as family we are called to love one another. This love applies not only to those in our local fellowship but to Christians around the world, including those who worship in different ways to us or*

are very different from ourselves culturally, and especially those who are suffering for their faith.

Now read verses 6-13.

In verses 6-8, Paul uses a number of specific gifts as illustrations: prophecy, service, teaching, etc.

- Each Christian is called to make some specific contribution to the life of the community and to do so to the best of their ability. This contribution is called their 'ministry', the work for which God has particularly gifted and called us.
- We shall not necessarily discover this ministry immediately.
- Other Christians may be able to help us by telling us how they see God's gifts emerging in our lives.

This can be illustrated by thinking about a school. In many secondary schools, pupils begin by taking all the subjects in the curriculum. As they progress up the school, they take fewer and fewer subjects at greater depth. Eventually whether they go on to further education or employment, they may end up specialising in one particular area. As they progress, they will benefit from guidance from their teachers to find the right subjects to take.

Explore this in the context of your particular church. Consider the particular ministries which are being exercised. Don't make this too 'churchy'. Illustrate this with ministries being exercised in the community and the world as well as the church. People should be encouraged to 'have a go' without fear of failing. Part of being the family of the church is about allowing growth and experimentation in an atmosphere of support, encouragement and acceptance that sometimes things will go wrong.

- Whatever we are called to do we should tackle it with determination and enthusiasm (v. 11).
- Notice again the importance of love and respect for our fellow Christians (vv. 9-10). Remember that love can be very practical (v. 13).

Guidance

The question of 'How do I know what God wants me to do?' arises not just when it comes to discovering our gifts and ministries. It is an important question for the whole of our lives—e.g., work, marriage, family decisions. It is too big a topic to cover in detail now, but the beginning of Romans 12 gives us a good place to start.

Read Romans 12:1-2 and notice the final sentence, 'Then you will learn to know God's will for you.' In order to find God's will, we must first:

- Dedicate our lives to him (v. 1).
- Stop thinking in the world's way, i.e., 'Don't copy the behavior and customs of this world' (v. 2). (One translator says graphically, 'Don't let the world around you squeeze you into its own mould' [PHILLIPS].)
- Let God transform our thinking (v. 2). This happens as we study Scripture, pray, listen to Christian teaching and talk with one another.

In the Greek these verses are in the plural. God's will is often to be found in talking and praying with others and not in lonely struggling as an individual.

The Church Member

Here is your opportunity to talk about the importance of being fully involved in the local church.

The following may need adapting to your particular context, but don't shy away from topics you might find difficult like financial giving. The tone should be encouraging and supportive rather than legalistic.

It may be helpful, having adapted it to your context, to print out the following and hand it out to all group members. Our version is in the Journal but they could be encouraged to put your church-specific version alongside it or pasted over it. (An adaptable version is available to download from the website https://saintsalivecourse.com.)

Go through the handout together inviting comment and discussion. Help members to see that belonging to the church involves much more than occasionally turning up to worship when we need help or can't think of anything better to do!

Whilst it is good if people feel able to sign this commitment, it is important not to put them under pressure to do so. You will be aware of the particular circumstances of group members. They should only promise things which it is realistic for them to be able to fulfil. Some may need to discuss aspects of it with their families. Suggest that signing it is something they might like to do later and then bring it to the final session. If it has been decided to present this commitment in some way to the whole church family, tell them that you will provide a further copy for this so they can keep the original.

I, _____,
have decided before Christ that I will seek his help to be a loyal
member of _____ Church.
As a loyal member I will:

- Be regular in worship and prepare for it with care.
- Join with others in fellowship, prayer and study.
- Give care and practical help to others, both members of the church and those outside, especially to those in the greatest need.
- Give regular financial support to the church.
- Seek to discover and exercise the gifts God has given to me.
- Pray for other members of the church and especially for those in leadership.
- Accept and support the leadership—not unthinkingly but as a responsible adult.
- Avoid gossiping about or criticising others. Talking to people directly and not behind their backs.
- Continue to think about my faith and how it relates to my home, work, recreation and other parts of my life.
- Seek to share my faith with others by praying for them, looking for opportunities to speak to them and inviting them to church events or groups.

Signed_____ Date _____

This is a model commitment. All of us will find ourselves falling short on occasion. When this happens, recognise it, say sorry and carry on!

After the Course

How can we continue to grow in our faith and to build upon what we have received together as a group? What are our hopes and expectations as the course comes to an end? *Lead into a discussion about the future. This is an opportunity to share how members can be part of an ongoing small group. (Remember that it is far better if this group can stay together, at least for a while, rather than expect members who have grown close to each other to go and join other groups.)*

Many in the group may have enjoyed the journalling element in Saints Alive! There is a section at the end of this week's Journal notes about continuing to keep a Journal. *If any of the leaders keeps a Journal it might be helpful to bring it along and show the group—from a distance, of course, because what we put in our Journals is private! In any case it would be helpful to draw the attention of the group to this page.*

If the group would like one, you could take a group photo which could be printed off and given to every group member next week as a memento.

Prayer

By now the group should be able to pray and worship together freely. Spend some time thanking God for one another and what you have received during the course as individuals and a group. Pray about what has been discussed during this session and any particular needs which have been expressed. Leave space for God to speak and the gifts of the Spirit to be exercised.

Administration

Remind people that there is information in their Journals about where they can find resources to help with ongoing Bible study and prayer as well as the page about keeping a Journal.

Discuss arrangements for next week, whichever option has been chosen. (If a 'Party with a Purpose' has been decided upon, course members should already know about this so that they could invite family and friends.) Decide on what sort of food you want to have and who is going to bring what.

If you have decided to share Communion together, explain that it will be informal and in your usual meeting place.

Anglicans may note that while it is possible that some members of the group may not yet be confirmed they will almost certainly, in the words of the Book of Common Prayer, be 'ready and desirous' of confirmation and so may receive.

Session 9

CELEBRATING TOGETHER

Aims:

- To end the course with a party that celebrates all that has taken place in previous weeks.
- Either to make the link between ordinary meals and the special meal of the Lord's Supper or Holy Communion or to give an opportunity for evangelism among family and friends.

LEADING THE SESSION

The way in which the course ends should depend on the needs of the group members and the pattern of church life.

Two ways of finishing are offered here—one focusing on fellowship and the other on evangelism. There are other possibilities which churches have followed:

1. A party to which family members and friends are invited.
2. A more formal Eucharist with a meal afterwards.
3. A party for the whole church organised by course members.
4. Some social or evangelistic outreach which course members undertake together.

Options three or four could be organised in addition to the final session, encouraging group members to look outwards and offering them an opportunity to share their faith with others.

Option A: Shared Meal and Eucharist

Things to think about:

- Eat first or worship first?
- Same room or different rooms?
- Is another church leader joining you to preside at Communion?

The answers will probably be dictated by the practicalities.

Holy Communion (The Eucharist or Lord's Supper or Mass)

The service should be creative and informal with as much participation as possible. The very word 'eucharist' means 'thanksgiving' so this should flow naturally and joyfully from the meal. However, there is some value, especially for those who are not used to attending such a service, in following the pattern they will find in church without this becoming too formal. Most Communion services have a two-fold structure (word followed by meal), often with intercession forming the bridge between the two. In churches with a regular liturgy, it may be worth including some familiar prayers from the liturgy. If the group is used to singing together, make sure you include some suitable songs or hymns. The following is a possible way to structure this part of the evening:

- *Explain briefly what will happen and link this with the structure of your usual Communion service.*
- *Begin with a time of praise and worship.*
- *Read a suitable passage from the Bible (e.g., part of John 6 or Acts 2:42-47) and spend a little while talking about it together. This is Bible study, not a sermon.*
- *Have a time of open prayer focusing on themes from the reading and looking outwards to pray for the church and the world.*
- *Read the narrative of institution from 1 Corinthians 11:23-26 or use one of the Eucharistic prayers used in your church.*
- *Say the Lord's Prayer together. (The text is in the Journal on page 18.)*
- *Share the bread and wine with one another, passing it around the circle. Either use the words common in your church or have the leaders say the words on behalf of everyone and pass the bread and wine in silence.*

- *Lead into a time of thanksgiving for God's blessings and pray for each course member by name, possibly with the laying on of hands.*
- *Have one of the leaders pray a prayer of blessing.*
- *If it is part of your tradition, it can be good to finish by sharing the Peace together.*
- *Add a final word of encouragement to 'go on being filled with the Spirit' (Ephesians 5:18), emphasising that a constant filling results in a constant outpouring to the world. Or in the words of Ignatius of Loyola, 'Go forth and set the world on fire!'*

Option B: Evangelistic 'Party with a Purpose'

This needs to be carefully planned and executed.

- *Decide at the outset whether the purpose of the meeting is directly evangelistic or to encourage people to come on the next course. It has usually been found that the latter is best. If so it would be helpful to invite the leaders of the next course, if they are going to be different from this one, to join you.*
- *By Session 8, but probably earlier, course members should have been asked to invite friends and relatives. You may have produced special invitations.*
- *Course members should let leaders know how many people they are expecting to bring. If an alternative venue is needed, it should not be too big and should be well*

prepared beforehand with the help of church members. (A bit of a crush is better than rattling around in a church hall and helps people talk to one another.)
- The leaders should set an example by inviting people who have expressed an interest in coming on a Saints Alive! course or who have shown an interest in exploring faith. But the main responsibility for inviting people should rest with course members.
- Encourage course members to see themselves as the hosts and take responsibility for welcoming and entertaining their guests.
- The meal should be prepared in advance so no one is unduly tied up in the kitchen.
- After the meal and a relaxed time for talking, a few members could be asked to say what being on the course has meant for them. Contributions should not be too long—an interview where the leader or another member of the group asks questions can keep things moving.
- The leaders should then outline the nature of the course. You can use some of the material from the Introductory Meeting. Prepare a card to give out sharing the start date of the next course and contact details for those who wish to find out more.
- Give course members responsibility for following up with the people they bring. If they want to accompany them to the next course that is fine as they will get something different out of it next time round.

Administration (following either option)

Make it absolutely clear what is happening next. If the group is continuing to meet, remind them when and where. If members are to join other groups, let them know who their link person will be and when and where those groups are meeting. Whichever option you follow, it is worth putting this information in writing so people don't forget.

Emphasise that they can approach you at any time for advice or help. Say that you would love to meet again in about three months with each group member, like you did before Session 6, just to see how they are getting on, but that you expect to see them regularly in worship or social gatherings anyway. (Make a note in your diary to remind you to contact them!)

Encourage them, if they have enjoyed the course, to recommend it to others. This does more than help you recruit for the next course, it helps them begin to witness.

If some group members are to be baptised, received into membership or confirmed, make sure everyone knows when and where that will happen so they can all be there to support one another.

Send them on their way rejoicing!

APPENDIX

Becoming a Christian— Christian Initiation

How do you become a Christian, and where does it all fit into Saints Alive!?

When leading a Saints Alive! group, questions about the relationship between different approaches to thinking about and experiencing God often arise. It may be helpful to use this 'Hexagon of Faith' which tries to draw together the different New Testament strands and also the different traditions within the church.

The Hexagon of Faith

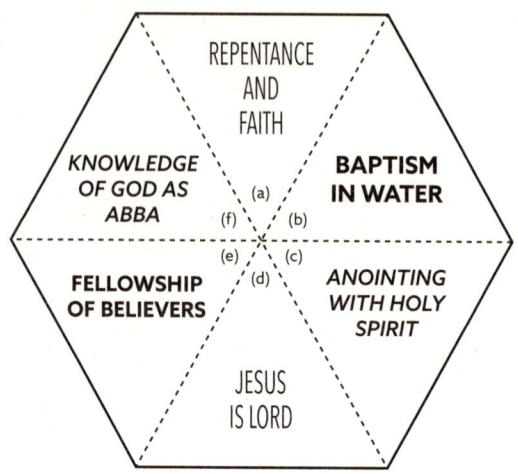

In the New Testament there are at least six different facets to becoming a Christian:

a) Repentance and faith—the conscious turning away from sin to God in response to the preaching of the cross (Mark 1:15; Acts 2:38; 3:19).

b) Baptism in water (Acts 2:38-41; 10:47; Romans 6:3).

c) Being filled with the Holy Spirit (sometimes called being anointed or baptised in the Spirit) (Acts 2:38-41; 10:44-48; 11:15-17; 1 Corinthians 12:4-11).

d) Confessing Jesus as Lord (Romans 10:9; 1 Corinthians 12:3; Philippians 2:11).

e) Joining the fellowship of believers—the church (Acts 2:41-47; 1 Corinthians 12:12-13).

APPENDIX

f) Knowing God as Abba ('Father') and being adopted as a child in his family (Romans 8:14-16; Galatians 4:5-7). Some would wish to integrate these with justification (Romans 5:1) and assurance (Ephesians 1:7).

As we look at these six facets, we can see that our full response to the grace of God shown to us in Christ is through:

- (a) and (d)—personal commitment to God
- (b) and (e)—corporate belonging to the church
- (c) and (f)—openness to the Holy Spirit

Different people enter into the Christian life through different facets of the diagram. None is possible without the finished work of Christ and the prior working of the Holy Spirit in the individual.

As is clear from the biblical references, these elements are inextricably interwoven and taken together to form a whole. This is shown in the diagram by the dotted lines between the facets—it is possible and desirable that people move freely from one to the other. There will be different emphases for different people, but this must never be allowed to destroy the unity of God's design for each of us.

The way in which this happens in the life of each individual varies wonderfully according to circumstance, personality and the work of the Holy Spirit in their lives. It can vary:

- ***Chronologically.*** The six facets can happen in any order. Martha may have been baptised as an infant, grown up in the fellowship of the church, come to a personal relationship with Christ through repentance and faith in her teens and experienced the power of the Spirit in her thirties. Mark may have had an overwhelming experience of the power of God as an adult that only later leads to church membership and baptism.

- *Experientially.* One aspect may initially be far more significant than another. Joshua may have had a dramatic conversion while Joan looks back with joy to her powerful filling with the Holy Spirit. (Many find that with the passage of time and the discovery of new facets of truth, past experiences come to have new significance.)
- *Theologically.* These different facets belong together. Perhaps one could say that Christian initiation is incomplete until a disciple has begun to enter into and appreciate all six. For many, the filling of the Holy Spirit is the key which gives a deeper appreciation of all the rest.

Saints Alive! has been written with the conviction that repentance and faith and the anointing with the power of the Holy Spirit belong together. Therefore there is no attempt to lead people into a prayer of commitment at the end of Session 2 when we have been speaking of the life and death of Jesus. Ministry is reserved for Session 6 when commitment to Christ is linked with praying for the infilling of the Holy Spirit. We are also convinced that the New Testament knows nothing of the lone Christian. Jesus' invitation to the disciples to follow him was at the same time a call to join the community of disciples. This is explored in Sessions 7 and 8.

In Saints Alive! the phrase 'being filled with the Spirit' is used as shorthand to talk about what is sometimes called the 'anointing' or 'release' or 'baptism' of the Holy Spirit. We believe that the phrase expresses something very important—the complete surrender of body, mind and spirit to be filled to the brim with the glory of God and the power that flows from him.

In an age which too often sees a Christian as a do-gooder or just as someone interested in religious things, we should not water down the way of the cross and what that means in discipleship. For some the laying on of hands with prayer in Session 6 will be a powerful and immediately life-transforming experience. For others it will be a quiet but no less significant opening up to God. For some there will be tears or laughter, tongues or prophecy, while others will receive a deep assurance of God's presence and peace. God tailors our experiences of himself to meet our personal needs.

The Church

Inevitably in Saints Alive! groups, questions arise about the church—its life and our differences and controversies.

We have found that the hexagon diagram is a most useful tool to help people to understand the different emphases and traditions in the church.

The differences between these three aspects of discipleship have had enormous (and expensive) implications for the life of the whole church. Broadly speaking:

- (a) and (d)—Protestants have focussed on personal commitment and have evangelised through preaching. They have built a myriad of churches to enclose pulpits from which to proclaim Christ.
- (b) and (e)—Catholics have focussed on corporate belonging and evangelised through sacrament and education. They have built innumerable schools in which to bring up the young in the faith.
- (c) and (f)—Pentecostals have focussed on the Holy Spirit and evangelised by offering ministry—often through the laying on of hands.

Differences are also discernible in the distinctions we make between the persons of the Trinity. Protestants tend to emphasise the person of Jesus and in particular his work of atonement at Calvary. Catholics tend to look to the Father and the wonder of creation and the importance of the incarnation at Bethlehem. Pentecostals emphasise the working of the Holy Spirit and the experience of Pentecost.

But God is one—Father, Son and Holy Spirit—and it takes the whole church to evangelise the whole world.

The approach taken in this Appendix does not claim to answer all the theological questions surrounding Christian initiation. Our concern in writing Saints Alive! is that people enter more fully into their

APPENDIX

inheritance in Christ and are empowered and gifted for their service in the world. Terminology is of secondary importance. Nevertheless, the model set out here is one which we believe reflects the complementary strands within the New Testament and something of the mystery of the Trinity.

Whether scribbled on a piece of paper or more formally presented in a lecture room, this diagram and its explanation have been found helpful to many, and they are offered on that basis. We need to make each facet our own and keep it fresh.

RESOURCE

Alive in the Spirit and Active in Mission

ReSource for Anglican Renewal Ministries helps little, local and ordinary churches to engage with the Holy Spirit for renewal, discipleship and mission.

ReSource's vision is for churches of all traditions, shapes and sizes to be alive in the Spirit and active in mission.

"ReSource were excellent! Biblical depth alongside openness to the Holy Spirit and relevant to ordinary church life and my calling to ministry. Real and Honest. Inspiring and refreshing"

Get in touch

ReSource works on the ground locally, to serve churches and support church leaders. **For more information about Renewal events, Church weekends, Sanctuary Days, the Alongside companionship scheme and online Resources Hub visit:**

www.resource-arm.net or contact
ReSource, Meeting Point House, Telford, TF3 4HS,
or **office@resource-arm.net**